CONSTRUCTING RACE

SUNY series, Power, Social Identity, and Education

Lois Weis, editor

CONSTRUCTING
R A C E

Youth, Identity, and
Popular Culture in South Africa

NADINE E. DOLBY

STATE UNIVERSITY OF NEW YORK PRESS

Cover art is by Clifford Barratt, a grade 12 student living in Durban, South Africa.

Published by
STATE UNIVERSITY OF NEW YORK PRESS, ALBANY

© 2001 State University of New York

For information, address State University of New York Press,
90 State Street, Suite 700, Albany, NY 12207

Production and book design, Laurie Searl
Marketing, Anne M. Valentine

Library of Congress Cataloging-in-Publication Data

Dolby, Nadine, 1964–
    Constructing racialized selves : youth, identity, and popular culture in
South Africa/Nadine Dolby
        p. cm. — (SUNY series, power, social identity, and education)
    Includes bibliographical references and index.
    ISBN 0-7914-5081-3 (alk. paper) — ISBN 0-7914-5082-1 (pbk. : alk. paper)
    1. South Africa—Social conditions—1994- . 2. Youth—South Africa—
Social conditions. 3. South Africa—Race relations. 4. South Africa—Ethnic
relations. 5. Blacks—Race identity—South Africa. 6. Whites—Race
identity—South Africa. 7. Colored people (South Africa)—Race identity.
8. Popular culture—South Africa. I. Title. II. Series.

DT1756 .D65 2001
305.8'00968—dc21   00-054910

10   9   8   7   6   5   4   3   2   1

Contents

Foreword 1

Acknowledgements 5

CHAPTER ONE
RETHINKING SELVES: IDENTITIES AND CHANGE 7

CHAPTER TWO
HISTORICAL FRAMES: APARTHEID, IDENTITY, AND SCHOOLING 19

CHAPTER THREE
DAILY LIFE AT FERNWOOD 31

CHAPTER FOUR
SHIFTING GROUND:
THE CHANGING CONTEXT OF RACE AT FERNWOOD 47

CHAPTER FIVE
CREATING RACE:
THE ROLE OF TASTE IN YOUTH'S PRODUCTION OF IDENTITIES 63

CHAPTER SIX
BORDERWORK: CONFLICT AND CONNECTION 79

CHAPTER SEVEN
THE TEXTURE OF THE BORDER:
PORTRAITS OF INDIVIDUAL STUDENTS 95

CHAPTER EIGHT
THE FUTURES OF RACE 111

Appendix. Negotiating Place:
Reflections on Method, Theory, and Being There 119

Notes 133

References 139

Index 151

FOREWORD

Two particularly powerful sets of ideas guide Nadine Dolby's remarkable study of youth and identity formation in contemporary post-apartheid South Africa. These ideas have to do with the theoretical status and practical operation of the concepts of culture and race in the dynamically changing educational and social contexts of modern nation-states. The crucible of study, here, is the South African context. But what Dolby discovers and brings to the level of intense scrutiny and reflexivity has broad application to a central issue confronting educational systems around the globe: the challenge of diversity and multiplicity as the rapid movement of people, ideas, images, and economic and cultural capital now bears down upon modern subjects and the social and cultural institutions that govern and regulate their lives.

First, Dolby maintains, based on her investigations of the radically hybrid and eclectic uses of popular culture by South African school youth, that the present usage of the term "culture" in educational theory and practice simply has to be rethought. Indeed, though pivotal to contemporary curriculum discourses such as multiculturalism, "culture" is significantly undertheorized and often treated in various curricular applications as a rigidly bounded set of values and linguistic or folkloric practices. Culture within this formulation becomes the organizing principle and final property of particular groups. Dolby argues instead that a more useful way to think about culture is to be found in the cultural studies formulations of Stuart Hall (1991, 1992) and David Morley and Kevin Robins (1995). Culture is better thought of, these writers insist, not as a unity, entity, or deposit, but as a set of processes imbricated in the production and circulation of images and as a site of the elaboration of identities in the new globalizing context that has overtaken modern nation-states. This approach now links the work of culture in education to other sites of mediation of the needs, interests, and desires of contemporary youth: popular culture, public policy, and ultimately the vulnerable modern state apparatuses themselves.

Vitally related is Dolby's second set of provocative ideas, in which she offers new terms for understanding race and its operation within the radically transforming school contexts of modern South Africa. Here, she argues that the auratic status of race—that is, the notion of defining race by reference to "origins" or biological or cultural unity—has been broken, overwhelmed by the immense processes of hybridity unleashed in contemporary life. Migration, electronic mediation, and the work of imagination of ordinary people—in other words, the dynamic forces of globalization—have had the effect of separating culture from place as scholars such as Anthony Giddens and Arjun Appadurai have informed us. In this radical context of the integration of the global into the local and vice versa, difference has become an abstract value that can be extracted or skimmed off from specific groups and cultural settings and combined and recombined, narrated and renarrated, with new elements in ways that, for instance, allow clothing designer magnates like Tommy Hilfiger to appropriate aspects of inner-city hip hop culture and sell "hood"-like clothes back to the inner city itself and to the world.

The conceptual ground developed here is very significant indeed. In brief, we have new conceptualizations of culture and race that help us better address the complex realities that school youth and their teachers face as we enter the new millennium. But Dolby goes further in *Constructing Race*. She puts these sophisticated theoretical understandings to work in her study of a specific educational context: the complex uses of culture in the elaboration of racial identities among African, coloured, Indian, and white youth in a post-apartheid South African high school called Fernwood. Drawing on Pierre Bourdieu's theory of "taste" and social classification, Dolby argues that the practices of cultural selection and appropriation play a critical role in the production and reproduction of unequal racial identities among school youth in the "new" South Africa. While educational scholars typically treat race as the elaboration of essentialism and particularism, Dolby points to the radical alienation of South African youth from their local and national contexts and their paradoxical "openness" to the cultural offerings of the global arena. Ironically, these youth then use these new cultural forms—rap music associated with the US urban ghettos, Levi jeans and rave culture associated with suburban white youth of Europe and North America—to redraw lines of distinction among themselves that often cut at right angles to the old forms of affiliation linked to ethnic ancestry. Here, Dolby links the methodological purchase offered by Bourdieu's concept of taste to the globalization theory of the University of Chicago-based postcolonial anthropologist, Arjun Appadurai. Deploying the theory of globalization to understand the highly particularistic practices associated with racial identity formation in education is in fact a bold and highly innovative conceptual move. Indeed, the critical area of globalization research has pretty much remained on the margins of the educational field. And, the literature on globalization remains virtually unreferenced in the writings on race and education, even in the emergent scholarship of critical race theory. Dolby's unique insight here, based on her study of youth practices of identity formation at Fernwood, is that in the hypperreal, mass-mediated world in which we live today, "taste" may be displacing "culture" (understood as a unity of distinctive folkloric group practices) as the critical vehicle and carrier of social distinctions among South African and urban school youth throughout the modern world. In other words, group affiliation, among South African coloured youth, for example, may be more strongly determined by what brand-name American-made jeans you are wearing than where you or your ancestors come from. In this new context of globalization, fashion, style, ultimately "taste," compete with "ancestry" and "geography" as pivotal variables in the elaboration of youth identities.

This bold study of the new dynamics of race and culture in post-apartheid schooling in South Africa has important implications for modern educational theorists and practitioners in industrialized countries such as the United States. Put directly, contemporary curriculum thinkers and practitioners cannot any longer afford to look askance at critical developments associated with globalization now transforming social and cultural life outside and inside schools around the globe. These developments have enormous implications for pedagogical practice and the educational preparation of school youth. And, as Dolby demonstrates, the lack of reflexivity on these new dynamics of economy, culture, and identity can have enormous transitional costs for students and teachers alike. The great task of teachers and educators as we enter the new millennium is to address these new patterns of racial reconfiguration, cultural rearticulation, hybridity, and multiplicity now invading educational institutions in the new era of globalization. Against the tide of these developments, curriculum thinkers, particularly in the United States, have tended to draw down a bright line of distinction between the established school curriculum and the teeming world of multiplicity, hybridity, and plurality that now flourishes in the everyday lives of school youth beyond the school.

A fundamentally new direction is needed in the approach to culture, race, and identity as we enter the twenty-first century. This approach must begin by rejecting the simplistic practice of cultural essentialism that now governs the organization of knowledge in schooling, even in such areas as multicultural education. Such a new theoretical and practical direction must involve a radical rethinking of the linkages of knowledge, culture, and human experiences across cultural and geographical boundaries. For instance, we need to explore conscientiously the links between first world development and third world underdevelopment—the links between South Africa, for example, and Europe or the United States. This is a position that Latin American and African scholars such as André Gunder Frank, Benjamin Cardoso, and Samir Amin have been articulating for sometime. It means thinking relationally and contextually, as Dolby suggests. It means we must read back into educational discourses all those tensions and contradictions that we tend to suppress as we process experience and history into curricular knowledge. It means abandoning the auratic status of concepts such as culture, race, and identity for the recognition and affirmation of the vital cultural porosity that exists between and among all human groups in the modern world.

It means foregrounding and stimulating the intellectual autonomy of students by incorporating the open-mindedness and inquiry that comes from letting diverse traditions debate with each other under the new rubric that we learn most about ourselves by learning more about others. It means, ultimately, thinking across disciplinary boundaries and the insulation of knowledge, linking the syndical and the pedagogical in the work we do.

CAMERON McCARTHY

Acknowledgements

This book was made possible through the support and encouragement of numerous individuals over the past fifteen years. For initial inspiration, I need to thank Howard Zinn, one of my earliest teachers and mentors. Themba Vilakazi and Mokubung Nkomo, of what was then Fund for a Free South Africa, provided me not only with employment, but with an introduction and welcome to South Africa. Mokubung was particularly helpful at early stages of this work.

In South Africa, thanks to Johan Muller, Pam Christie, Roger Deacon, Rob Morrell, Nick Taylor, Alan Penney, Tansey Jessup, Crain Soudien, the South African Communication Service, Doug Bromley, and Keyan Tomaselli and the Centre for Cultural and Media Studies at the University of Natal for affiliation during this research. Of course, the individuals I need to thank most in Durban, the students and staff of Fernwood High School (and the other schools I visited), must remain anonymous. They generously let me into their lives during a turbulent, uncertain year for the school, and I am very thankful to them. The research was supported by a Fulbright grant. A travel grant from the Faculty of Education at Monash University supported a return trip to Fernwood in 1999.

Friends in South Africa who helped along the way include Leah and Elleck Nchabaleng, Faiza Salie, Leanne Westoby, and Arvin and Asha Bhana. The whole David family, too numerous to mention here by name, very quickly became my family and their support (particularly Florence and Stephen's) helped me through some of the difficult challenges of this research and daily life in South Africa.

Back in the United States, Cameron McCarthy never waivered in his support of me or this project, and his example is a continuing inspiration. Sonia Nieto, Warren Crichlow, Bill Martin, Kal Alston, Margery Osborne, and John (and Layne) St. Julien provided encouragement, critique, and friendship. The Center for African Studies at the University of Illinois (particularly Paul Tiyambe Zeleza and Prosper Godonoo) gave me an intellectual home and support of all kinds. My thanks of course also go to Lois Weis and SUNY Press, (especially Priscilla Ross and Laurie Searl) for their support and publication of this book. Rebecca Raby provided invaluable assistance with the index.

Friends who saw me through various stages of this project include Heriberto Godina, Shuaib Meacham, Wendy and Chris Burke, Leanna and David Blackmon, Natasha Levinson, Debbie Murphy, Kwaku Korang and Gifty Ako-Adounvo (and of course Kwame!), Ivor Emmanuel, Ishara Ramkisson and Surenderan Naiker (and Mishka), Karen and Mike Retzer, and Greg Dimitriadis. My family, particularly my mother, brother, grandmothers (Alice and Mae), Aunt Leslie, and Lynne supported me throughout. In the end, this book is for Stephen, who saw me through it all, and makes everything possible.

Chapter One

Rethinking Selves:

Identities and Change

L ife in the 1980s in South Africa was marked by increased and sustained polit-ical protests, strikes, boycotts, states of emergency, violent repression by the state, and finally, by the end of the decade, the anticipation of imminent and pro-found change. In the mid-1980s, in the midst of this ongoing war against the state, a new generation of children started school. In this generation's early childhood, many of the laws that defined apartheid were dismantled; by the time they were ten, Nelson Mandela was released from prison; as they entered adolescence, he became president and a democratic South Africa was established for the first time in history. The terrain on which these children grew, and continue to grow up, is substantially different from that of their parents and even older siblings. They are a generation whose past, present and future are neither completely defined by apartheid, nor completely free of it.

For a small, relatively elite group of these youth the dramatic political shifts of the early 1990s brought significant changes to their lives. When white [1] schools were allowed to admit black students in the early 1990s, a significant, though still relatively small number of South African children were schooled in multiracial environments for the first time in over forty years. Although white private schools had been desegregated since the mid-1970s, and Indian and coloured schools had admitted African students for at least a decade, the opening of white government schools provided the first widespread opportunity for African, coloured, Indian, and white children to be in constant, daily contact. This ethnographic study was conducted in 1996 at a school of this type: a formerly white, now multiracial school in Durban I will call Fernwood High School.

Established in the 1960s as an all boys school, Fernwood by the 1970s had become coed (which was and still is unusual for white schools in Durban) and had also acquired a reputation as a dumping ground for white students with poor academic and behavioral records. By the late 1980s, Fernwood's student body was shrinking quickly, as the number of whites leaving South Africa increased. Threatened repeatedly with closure, Fernwood was at the forefront of desegregation in the 1990s, and quickly acquired a local reputation as the "new South Africa" school. From 1991 to 1996 (the year of this study), Fernwood's black student population skyrocketed: from 11% to over 66% of a student population of 600. Most of these black students are African, with a small number of coloured (5-7%) and Indian (1%) students. [2] More than any other formerly white school in Durban, Fernwood is alive with racial conversation and conflict—it is one of the few arenas in Durban in 1996 where youth of different races interact intimately on a daily basis.

For the students at Fernwood, racial identity is no longer formed in relative isolation from other racial groups, but in constant conversation and conflict with those others. In a society still profoundly divided and defined by race, these students' lives are not mere reflectors of previous generations' battles and antagonisms; instead their identities and relationships are productive of the new terrain of race and racial politics. As Paul Willis (1990) comments in the case of black youth in Great Britain,

> But young black people can never look wholly to the prior generation for clues about how to develop their own identities. The experiences of the two generations differ, and some cultural commonalities with white youth must arise from their shared conditions of life—common experiences in the same streets and schools mediated by many of the same cultural media. (p. 8)

Following Willis' insights, I argue that youth at Fernwood do not look solely to the past, to the remnants of apartheid, to develop and define their identities. "Race" after apartheid is not simply a matter of discarding or embracing already formed racial positions, but of renegotiating it in a new context. Race, its significance as a ground for politics and a category for the organization of daily life, has been transformed. This is not to suggest that race does not dominate the material and imaginary world of South Africa, or that racisms (S. Hall, 1986) have disappeared, but that the meanings that youth at Fernwood ascribe to race have shifted.

Given this premise, this study is based on a number of questions that probe how students engage with and make meaning of "race" as a location of identity. To that end, I examine the following questions: what is the significance of race to youth at Fernwood; how is race both conceptualized and lived at school; what is the impact of new material and discursive conditions within South Africa on the significance of race as a site of identity; and what are the local and global contexts that shape the ways in which students rearticulate race? Race, of course, does not function in an isolated manner, but also interacts with other factors such as class—an aspect of the story that is taken up at various points, particularly in chapters 3 and 6.

Much of the school-based research on youth and identity has focused on the specific relationship between the school as an institution, the actors located within the site of the school (teachers, administrators, etc.), and students (see, e.g., Davidson, 1996, and in South Africa, Soudien, 1998). This study takes a slightly different approach to thinking about youth and identity. Fernwood serves as a critical context for students' play with the concept of race; its unique racial composition and dynamics provide the terrain for compelling tales of race and change in South Africa. And its particular dynamics (detailed in chapter 3) are a necessary and vital frame through which to read students' formation of race. However, while I use a school as the basis for this study, I am simultaneously mindful that formal schooling is increasingly marginalized and disconnected from the pulse of students' lives. For example, Henry Giroux (1994a, 1994b) argues that popular culture, not schools, is the primary pedagogical site for youth. In this study, I emphasize the site of the school to explore it as a space in which the tensions inherent in contemporary South African society are played out. However, to fully explore and understand students' engagement with race, it is necessary to look outside the school, to factors both local and global. Through the course of the study, the global context of popular culture emerges as a critical site for the negotiation of race: for the marking of racialized borders, and for their subsequent displacement and rearrangement.

RACIALIZED SELVES

Identity, as a discursive formation, is a predominant force in structuring political, social, and national relations at the beginning of the twenty-first century (Balibar & Wallerstein, 1991; S. Hall & du Gay, 1996; Mercer, 1990; Rajchman, 1995; Rutherford, 1990). By a discursive formation, I mean that categories of identification (i.e., race, gender, class, sexual orientation, etc.) are not pre-given, essential traits, but constitute an array of available cultural meanings and identities into which one places or sutures oneself, at the same time internalizing those meanings in an attempt to stabilize both oneself and the surrounding world. Available racial categories shift and move, contingent both on time and space (see e.g., S. Hall, 1998, for a discussion of the emergence of black as a political and cultural category).

Of particular concern for this book is the way that discourse makes, unmakes, and remakes racial positions. Commenting on the discursive power of racialized identities, Stuart Hall (1998) writes, "Not a question of what is true, but what is *made* to be true. Such is the way in which racial discourses operate. To use a familiar Foucault phrase, it is a 'regime of truth'" (p. 290, emphasis is the author's). Thus, racial identity's existence as a conceptual frame for the organization of human activity is not a naturalized state, or as Joan Scott (1995), comments a "condition of human existence" but is instead an "enunciation . . . that constitutes hierarchies and asymmetries of power" (p. 5).

Historically, as Michael Banton (1988) argues, the idea of "race" has shifted from emphasizing lineage within a philosophical and theological paradigm that traced all humans to God, to a scientifically grounded category that conceptualized race as biology. Couched in the language of scientific objectivity, the notion of biologically distinct categories—what Saul Dubow (1994) refers to as the "pseudoscience of race"—persists.

Alongside the discourse of biological racism, the discourse of "new racism" has gained strength in recent years. Instead of relying on biological conceptions of difference, new racism invokes immutable, essential cultural differences; race is signified through coded terminology—it is not directly named. This coding of race as culture has its roots in anthropological notions of race (or "culturalism"). At first, and in its context, culturalism had somewhat progressive aims—to combat "racial science" that deemed some cultures as primitive, and some peoples (predominantly black and brown) as needing the civilizing influence of Western (white) societies (Bennett, 1998). In contrast, culturalism argued that different races represented separate and distinct cultures that could not be compared or rated as more or less civilized or advanced. As "culturalism" has evolved, however, it has become what Etienne Balibar (1991) refers to as "racism without races," which he defines as

> a racism whose dominant theme is not biological heredity but the insurmountability of cultural differences, a racism which, at first sight, does not postulate the superiority of certain groups or peoples in relation to others but 'only' the harmfulness of abolishing frontiers, the incompatibility of lifestyles and traditions. (p. 21)

Paul Gilroy (1987) provides an extensive study of how "race," in the context of Thatcher's Great Britain, becomes coded as "culture," for example, in Margaret Thatcher's fear that Britain is being "swamped by people with a different culture," here referring to immigrants from India and Pakistan (Goldberg, 1992, p. 551).

Race's power derives not from its singularity, but from its multiplicity, and its remarkable ability to be reproduced and recirculated within ever-changing contexts.[3] Fernwood students encounter a peculiar and distinct moment in the history of "race," as the end of apartheid meets a world that is encountering a new, intensified form of globalization. For these students, part of the "work" of identity (Soudien, 1996) is to make sense of the meaning of race in a period in which the category is legally unhinged and subject to multiple discursive formations. Negotiating the marking and definition of racial difference is an all-absorbing and constant task at Fernwood.

THE GLOBAL CONTEXT OF IDENTITY

Globalization, specifically here in the case of South Africa, is not a new reality. Kate Manzo (1992a) argues that South Africa's position within a global political economy goes back more than 400 years:

> The territorial space that is called South Africa has long been articulated within a global political economy that has shaped its internal politics since 1652 when Jan Van Riebeeck established his outpost of the Dutch East India Company at the Cape of Good Hope . . . . The social whole within which South African subjectivities have been constituted is the global political economy, not the domestic state. (p. 27)

As Manzo suggests, the particular racial formation that was apartheid in South Africa did not spring fully formed from South African soil, but instead was constructed and existed in a global context (Also see Beinart & Dubow, 1995; Dubow, 1989; Mathieson & Attwell, 1998; Marx, 1998). Although South Africa during the later apartheid years was certainly isolated in some respects through boycotts and disinvestment campaigns, it can by no means be theorized and analyzed as a space that is unaffected by the global. In contrast, the reality that South Africa was the focus of international boycotts and economic sanctions points not to its isolation, but to its central role in world politics.

In the realm of culture, David Coplan (1985), Stephen David (1996), Ulf Hannerz (1994), and Rob Nixon (1994) chart the historical influence of global popular culture on South Africa, particularly black South Africa. Nixon, for example, examines the ways in which the blossoming of artistic expression in Sophiatown in the 1950s draws on the Harlem Renaissance of the 1920s. Simultaneously, South African tsotsis (gangsters) of the 1950s turned to Hollywood movies to make fashion and style choices, and in turn to construct subjectivities. Blake Modisane (1965) remembers the influence of global fashion:

> The well-dressed man about Sophiatown was exclusively styled with American and English labels unobtainable around the shops of Johannesburg. . . . Shoes from America—Florsheims, Winthrops, Bostonians, Saxone and Mansfield from London; BVD's, Van Heusen, Arrow shirts; suits from Simpsons, Hector Powe, Robert Hall; Dobbs, Woodrow, Borsolino hats. The label was the thing. (p. 52)

As will become apparent in later chapters, potential parallels can certainly be drawn between the use of global popular culture in the 1950s and students' use of similar commodities in the 1990s. As Hannerz (1994, p. 190) argues, "It seemed that one would leapfrog over white South Africa, and involve oneself more directly with what one thought of as interesting, attractive or superior in more distant places." Despite Hannerz's acknowledgement of the influence of the global on black South Africans in the 1950s, he does little to engage with the meaning of those commodities within individuals' or communities' "mattering maps" (Goldstein, 1983). In the ethnographic portion of this book, I will not simply map the fact that global commodities populate students' lives, but argue that these artifacts of the popular take on specific, racialized meanings within their lives: that the global intimately shapes students' play with the local, lived reality of race.

Despite globalization's constancy, its particular form changes dramatically through the course of the twentieth century. Historically, the nation-state was the

locus for global relations, which were dominated by the dynamics of center/periph-
ery, colonizer/colonized, victor/vanquished, oppressor/victim, as the world rotated
around the axis of first Great Britain, and then the United States. Cultures, ideologies, ways of life, and economic and political systems were not shared, but were
generally imposed and enforced. The postcolonial world of 1996 bears the scars of
this history, as globalization takes on new, varied, and more complex characteris-
tics. The rise in transnational corporations that no longer feel allegiance to one
particular nation-state, and who in large measure wield significantly more economic
power than the vast majority of national entities, has changed the ability of any
one nation-state to solely determine its own destiny. Although there are of course
still vast differences in economic opportunity between the nations of what are often
labeled the "First World" and the "Third World," in the future, corporations, more
than nation-states, may define the hardships and opportunities of people's lives. As
George Lipsitz (1994) writes, ". . . the ability of any one nation state to determine
its people's life chances has become greatly constrained" (p. 28). While the nation-
state still controls, to a large extent, the movement of its citizens and the sanctity
of its borders, it has been increasingly overpowered by transnational corporations
that can more swiftly and directly impact lives. Both poor and rich states often position themselves in the service of transnational corporations, putting the needs of
capital over and above the needs of their citizens. For wealthy states these actions
are a matter of choice, yet poorer states find themselves entangled in a global net
controlled by a matrix of corporate and supranational bodies, which renders
questionable their sovereignty as independent states.

    While the cracks in the formation of the nation-state may be felt world-
wide, newly emerging democracies such as South Africa face specific and substantial problems in forging national identities. Although the South African
nation-state may be in the midst of reshaping itself as a political entity both at
home and in the larger global playing field, it holds only a minor, and often
insignificant, role in the ways that many youth in my study imagine their identities. For example, while African students are almost uniformly glad that
apartheid has been abolished, their satisfaction with this new reality does not
necessarily translate into allegiance to the nation. For a small, but significant,
minority, the previous government, led by then-president F. W. deKlerk, is understood as the force behind the end of apartheid; these students' allegiances lie with
them and against the government of Nelson Mandela and its desire to create a
nonracial nation. Other youth blame the ANC (African National Congress)-led
government for South Africa's economic problems; these youth value their
increased opportunities for education, though solely as a way of acquiring mar-
ketable skills that will allow them to leave South Africa. While it is doubtful that
many of these students will have the ability and resources to actually leave, and
many who do will come back, it is significant that South Africa does not constitute their "imagined community" (Anderson, 1991)—the nation-state is not a
primary point of identification and belonging. Few students have allegiance to

South Africa, and most say that they would readily move to other countries for better jobs, opportunities, and lives. President Mandela's continual calls for a "new patriotism" have little resonance at Fernwood High (Mandela, 1996).

In an attempt to retheorize the emerging global world, Arjun Appardurai (1990, 1996) identifies five "scapes," which he describes as the global flows of people, images, technology, capital, and ideologies. The South African youth in my study are situated, in most aspects of their lives, on the periphery of the global flows identified by Appadurai. Poor, working class, and lower middle class, they lack the economic resources that would allow them to materially exist in the center. Many Fernwood students look with longing towards the United States and Europe as the hub of life. I observed some students walking around school in a trance-like state, dreaming of their imagined future lives as Hollywood producers. Others aspire to leave South Africa to become au pairs (nannies) in Europe or the United States, and forge a better life there. Still others incessantly questioned me about life in the United States, opportunities for college, and details about the lives of movie stars. Globalization most clearly does not translate into equalization of resources. As Doreen Massey (1993) points out, everyone does not have the same access to global flows. While some, primarily the ruling transnational capitalist class and the intelligentsia, have control of these flows, others, for example, poor rural people in Africa or the urban working class in the United States, are on the receiving end. Although it may not be as clear which nations or entities are the center and which are the periphery, it is abundantly evident that the economic resources of the planet are unequally divided.

This does not, however, mean that Fernwood students are only on the receiving end of global flows. In contrast, as I will demonstrate in later chapters, the students are also active participants in the *creation* of the dynamics of globalization. However, this creation must be situated within its particular context, so that it is understood as a framework for interpreting identity, not an uncritical celebration of the cultural dominance of U.S. and European popular culture in South Africa.

Identity, then, can be understood as a constant process of formation and change that occurs within a global/local matrix, and that is both formed by and expresses structures of power. (Grossberg, 1996; Gupta & Ferguson, 1997a; Jameson & Miyoshi, 1998; King, 1991; Morley & Robins, 1995; Wilson & Dissanayake, 1996). My emphasis on the "global" does not discount the impact of the immediacy of the local—for example, the significance of growing up in a township with constant violence and death. Instead, interpreting identity within a global milieu signals that global forces impact the ways in which youth situate themselves within the local reality. For example, a young person may interpret the violence of the township not as a local condition of poverty, hopelessness, or political fighting, but as a global situation that is contiguous to the violence of South Central Los Angeles portrayed in rap songs. Understood in this framework, student comments such as "That's just the way things are," reflect more than anger and frustration at a local reality, but despair at what is viewed as a global condition.

Using and extending Appadurai's theoretical frame, it is possible to interpret how Fernwood students' lives are situated within, affected by, and also create the global flows that he identifies (and some that he does not, such as violence). Yet in terms of conscious, active engagement, it is the global flow of popular culture that captivates students' desires and energies, and so it is the focus of my analysis. The global popular is the predominant, though certainly not sole, lense through which Fernwood students come to understand themselves and their relationship to the "other" in a racially tense and divided school.

IDENTITY AND POPULAR CULTURE

Throughout this book, I will emphasize popular culture as a location or a "site" (Foucault, 1972) for identity formation. By using the concept of a site I underline that popular culture (or any other site) is not a solid, fixed object, but instead an ever-changing network of movement, which is structured by and through apparatuses of power, and is itself a result of struggle.

Popular culture is not usually understood or considered as a site for identity formation in ethnographic studies, and thus I want to elaborate on its position within the lives of students and its significance for my argument. [4] For students, popular culture is an integral part of their everyday experiences (McCarthy et al., 1999; Wilson-Brown & McCarthy, 1995). The importance of student experience, as Giroux and Roger Simon (1989) argue, is one of the benchmarks of radical education. The concepts of "empowerment" and "giving voice" demand in principle that adults listen to youth and their hopes, desires, and affective investments.

Despite this emphasis on student experience, educational research, particularly ethnographic educational research, has generally avoided engaging with a major source of student interest and investment: popular culture. Although there is an increasing focus on the analysis of popular culture texts (Dent, 1992; Giroux, 1994b; Steinberg & Kincheloe, 1997), there is much less scholarship that examines how youth make meaning from these texts, and the ways in which they enact those meanings in their lives. [5] This research attempts to address this gap by examining, as Angela McRobbie (1994) suggests, "the ongoing relations which connect everyday life with cultural forms" (p. 184). Research in this area is important not simply because popular culture is a formative arena for identity, but because popular culture is also an arena for political struggle. As S. Hall (1981) writes:

> Popular culture is one of the sites where this struggle for and against a culture of the powerful is engaged; it is also the stake to be won or lost in that struggle. It is the arena of consent and resistance. It is partly where hegemony arises, and where it is secured. (p. 239)

Popular culture is a key site for the formation of identities, for the ways in which we make sense of the world, and locate ourselves within it (Grossberg, 1989). It is intricately woven into our lives; it surrounds us, influencing the way we map our realities, imagine our possible lives, and relate to others. Popular culture has become, in Willis' (1990) words, "common culture." For youth at Fernwood, popular culture consumes large amounts of energy both in and out of school. Notebooks and pencil boxes are plastered with pictures of musical groups and movie stars, conversation is dominated by the latest dance craze, and on the field at lunchtime enterprising students sell sips of their Cokes (and their CDs, jewelry, and anything else they can find) to raise money to go to a concert. Students desire to model their lives not on Nelson Mandela (who arguably is a pop icon on his own—but perhaps more so outside of South Africa), but on the lives of Michael Jordan, Oprah Winfrey, and the cast of *New York Undercover*. Given that popular culture consumes substantial amounts of students' time and affective investment, identities, as Lawrence Grossberg argues, are largely determined within this space. That the enactment of these identities (and the very bounds of the imagination of these same identities) is constrained by local material realities is unquestioned; it is doubtful that any students at Fernwood High School will attain the stature of Jordan or Winfrey. But that is irrelevant to Grossberg's main argument, that popular culture must be both acknowledged and problematized as a site that *matters*.

Through emphasizing popular culture, I do not mean to diminish the impact of other sites on youth's identity formation. However, it is striking how popular culture (not church, family, neighborhood, or "traditional" culture) becomes the ground on which race is negotiated at Fernwood. This does not mean that other influences are unimportant, or that they do not shape students' lives. But in the public arena of Fernwood, popular culture becomes a way for students to think through and about race using what Willis (1990) terms "symbolic creativity." Youth at Fernwood invest meaning in this world of images and surfaces. As I interpret their daily interactions with the world of the popular, my guiding assumption is that youth are not passive receptors for an undifferentiated onslaught of corporate generated popular culture, but instead carefully select, mold, and combine specific commodities and other aspects of popular culture to create identities that are always contextualized within particular circumstances. Here, I take Willis' concept of "symbolic creativity" one step further, as I argue that for youth at Fernwood affective investments in popular culture become racialized, contextualized within the forces of contemporary South Africa, and intertwined with local racial and class dynamics.

At Fernwood, these investments also become the primary ground for conflict and struggle at the school. Race is defined and determined through attachments to particular aspects of popular culture, and identities, both in connection and conflict, are played out on this terrain. Popular culture is foregrounded as a terrain of struggle, from the school fashion show, to the music played at school events such as dances to school sports.

MAPPING RACE: THE DYNAMIC OF TASTE

Using popular culture as a fulcrum, this book develops and illustrates the argument that youth at Fernwood construct race primarily as a discourse of taste

(Bourdieu, 1984), whose coordinates are situated within the parameters of popular culture. I use the concept of taste, instead of the more familiar idea of culture, first to signal my move away from the commonsense trappings of "culture." In doing so, I position myself not against Pierre Bourdieu and his use of culture (for his use of culture, and notion of habitus, informs my own theorizing), but instead distinguish my analysis of "cultural" identity from its common use within much (though not all) educational literature. Although the idea of "cultures" as stable, bounded, separate entities has been thoroughly overturned in the academy (Clifford & Marcus, 1986; Gupta & Ferguson, 1997a; S. Hall & du Gay, 1996; Rosaldo, 1993), such paradigms still hold powerful sway in discussions of schooling and youth identities. As Norma González (1999) argues, "...while anthropologists may bemoan the essentialization and reification of bounded and shared cultural traits, the reality is that academic critical discourses have been slow to penetrate curricular practices in schools" (p. 431). By using Bourdieu's idea of taste, I switch the focus away from the essences of cultural identity, and towards what James Clifford (1988) refers to as the "processes" of identity. Second, such essentialist cultural paradigms posit a homology between a "people" and a "place." Our ideas of culture are tied to geography and to territory, even as we struggle to retheorize a world in which these links are weakened (if they ever existed in a "real" sense). Taste, in contrast, allows me to interpret race through a paradigm that is significantly more deterritorialized. By using taste, I do not jettison the specific context of South Africa and the cultural fields in which students maneuver. Instead, I mean to signal that race is significantly (though never entirely) divorced from a specific and narrow geographical place; instead, race is formed through the global/local nexus of taste practices, which are then given life in the particular context of Fernwood. Finally, through using the paradigm of taste, I also mean to reverse naturalized understandings about race. In educational literature, culture is often understood as an *expression* of a particular racial or ethnic group. This formulation, however, ultimately leads us back to an essentialist way of thinking, which postulates that identity is formed through "some authentic common origin or structure of experience" (Grossberg, 1994). By focusing on taste *practices*, and how these practices serve to actually *create and recreate* race, I break with models that assume that particular (cultural) practices are inherently tied to a specific group. The rapidly changing geography of taste at Fernwood allows me to probe how these practices are not naturally the "property" of any one racial group, but are essentially unstable. Furthermore, I can then examine how the *practices themselves* function to reshape racial identities.

Although taste becomes a way for Fernwood students to imagine and live race, taste in itself is not fixed. While culture, and cultural paradigms are certainly dynamic, taste at Fernwood is even less stable. As desperately as students try to erect and police racial borders based on taste, these borders change and mutate. What defines "coloured, "white," and "African," is not constant, but begins to shift, even in the relatively short time (one school year) of this study. Class dynamics also work themselves into the constitution of racialized taste patterns, as shifts in the class composition of Fernwood at different grade levels impact the formation and movement of taste divisions.

Despite the racially divisive atmosphere of Fernwood, there are students, and groups of students, who tinker with the borders of identity. Spaces of hybridity, border crossing, and a "play" with race may not flourish in every corner of Fernwood, but their mere existence troubles the simplistic picture of a school whose *only* dynamic is racial separation. Predominantly, these breaks and ruptures play themselves out through the dynamics of taste; clothes, music, and clubs are the practices through which students both define and then violate racial commonsense in Gramsci's terms. At times, global popular culture works in concert with local conditions to create temporary points of affiliation, shared desires, and investments, which allow alliances to develop between particular individuals or racial groups in the school. In this case, global flows are critical to understanding identity formation and political struggle at Fernwood, as global popular culture becomes the way that students actively engage race.

Interpreting "race" as taste does not diminish its force, nor is it an argument for "the end of racism." Instead, it points to the ever-changing dynamics of race, and highlights a potentially potent configuration of race that responds to a changing global situation. The common ground of urbanization, modernity, and increasingly, postmodernity produces a situation within which older discursive constructions of race cannot stand. Biology, culture, and history lose their force, as youth meet in a school saturated with dynamics that are markedly different than those that existed a generation ago.

OUTLINE OF CHAPTERS

To the end of understanding how race functions as a dynamic of taste within Fernwood, chapter 2 provides a historical framework and situating of the dynamics of racial identity and schooling in South Africa. I sketch an overview of schooling before and during apartheid, discuss "race" as it functioned both within South African society and the system of schooling, and then focus on the changes that begin to take place as apartheid is dismantled through the 1980s and 1990s. I draw on recent scholarship on multiracial schools from the 1970s onward both to provide the reader with the larger picture of desegregation in South African schooling and to mark out how this study deviates from previous research.

Having provided a broad historical frame, chapter 3 explores the specific history and politics of Fernwood High School and its process of desegregation through the 1990s. Initially Fernwood is one of the first white schools in Durban to desegregate, and its large black population (comparative to other white schools) earns it the reputation as the "rainbow" school. But by 1996 it is no longer a sunny representation of South Africa's possibility, but an exemplar of the tensions that crisscross South African society. In this chapter, teachers, management, and students speak to their experiences of daily life at Fernwood and the multiple collisions that frame their interactions.

The first half of chapter 4 examines the institutional structures and practices of race at Fernwood, through an examination of how the management and teachers at the school construct "black" and "white" through their practices. Students' confrontation with race and change is discussed in the second half of the chapter, as I use interview data to examine students' responses to discourses such as the new South Africa, and the material conditions of violence and death that envelop Durban in the mid-1990s. Race's constant presence at Fernwood assures that it will not disappear, be submerged under a discourse of nonracialism, or melt into a liberal celebration of difference. Instead, race persists, though, as I argue, its form and meaning change.

Students' production of race at Fernwood is the focus of chapter 5, which examines the conflicting dynamics of taste. Here, I elaborate on Bourdieu's notion of habitus and discuss its relevance to the analysis of racialized taste practices at Fernwood. I use taste to interpret the racial, and in some instances, class dynamics at Fernwood, demonstrating how Fernwood students use fashion and music to construct racialized selves and others and recreate local meanings of race that are inextricably bound to and within the global.

Using examples from everyday life and experiences at Fernwood, chapter 6 examines the conflicts and connections at the borders of racial relations within Fernwood. Conflict manifests itself through the setting and policing of racial taste borders and through the resentment (McCarthy et al., 1997) of white students towards their black classmates. Connections, though less common, are also evident, and again taste plays a formative role. Here, I examine how taste serves to help create divergent racial alliances among Fernwood students in grade 12 and grade 8. Chapter 6 also forefronts the ways in which class intersects with and influences the play of race at Fernwood, as shifting class dynamics influence the particular configurations of the connections that emerge both in grade 12 and grade 8.

Chapter 7 zeros in on the lives and experiences of seven individual Fernwood students, as I interpret how they negotiate the racial politics of the school. Each student profiled takes a different approach to working the borders of race, and their experiences and lives exemplify tales of possibility, which focus our attention not on the what is and what was of race, but the potentialities for its future.

Chapter 8 looks at the future of race in educational research and pedagogy. In this concluding chapter, I argue that race and difference must be engaged, analyzed, and challenged through ways that expose how and why they matter, as part of the work of defusing their power.

CHAPTER TWO

HISTORICAL FRAMES:

APARTHEID, IDENTITY, AND SCHOOLING

Segregation in schooling in South Africa predates apartheid by almost 400 years, though "race" as a structuring concept of separation is not a constant. Following the arrival of the Dutch at the Cape in 1652, formal schooling coexisted with the traditional educational practices of indigenous societies. One of the first schools established by Europeans was founded by the Dutch East India Company, and initially enrolled white colonialist children, enslaved Africans, and local Africans. However, the Dutch Reformed Church raised objections to the schooling of free and not free children in the same school, and eventually separate schools were established. The distinction here was not "racial" in the modern sense of the word, but instead was based on one's position in society.

Mission schools, established in the 18th century, represented another attempt at racial integration in schooling. For African, Indian, and coloured children, mission schooling was the primary means of obtaining a Western education. Black, and a few white, children attended these schools, which provided desegregated classrooms, but with segregated dining and boarding facilities. Mission schools, overall, achieved excellent examination results, competing with and often surpassing the results of white schools (Horrell, 1963).

The growth of the mining industry in the late 1800s provided the beginning of segregationist policies that invoked the modern concept of race. Mine owners preferred to hire unskilled, underpaid, black labor, as opposed to skilled and semiskilled white labor, thus causing a small, but politically astute and experienced group of white workers to band together along racial lines to save their jobs. Skin color became an important line of division, as white workers' class and employment interests became synonymous with race (Davies, 1982; Jeeves, 1982). In 1906, the government stepped in to secure jobs outside of the mining industry for whites, thus preventing white unemployment. These policies, often referred to as job color bars, designated specific jobs for individuals of a particular race, thus spreading an ideology of segregation and inequality. [1] "Race" as a "scientific" concept also emerged at this time, via disciplines such as eugenics and anthropology (Manzo, 1992b).

Job color bar policies influenced the development of educational policies and practices in the 20th century (Cross & Chisholm, 1990). Natal, soon to be followed by the Cape, introduced government funding for schools based on policies of selective segregation. Following the Anglo-Boer war, free primary education for white children was instituted, part of a British policy to anglicize Afrikaner children. Numerous acts followed, including the Cape 1905 School Board Act, Smut's Education Act of 1907 (Transvaal), and the Hertzog's School Act of 1908 (Orange Free State), all of which provided for compulsory, and racially segregated, education for white children.

Concurrently, the report of the South African Native Affairs Commission in 1905 advocated geographical separation of the races, separate systems of political representation, and an inferior, fee-based, noncompulsory system of education for Africans. Segregationist policies reflected more than the racist perspectives of the British rulers of the time; they also guarded against the possibility of concerted political action between poor whites and poor blacks. As Michael Cross and Linda Chisholm argue (1990), "Through education, white workers and youth were to be politically and ideologically incorporated into a white state to absorb and mute rising social and cultural conflicts" (p. 47).

The next several decades witnessed the consolidation and refinement of the system of segregated schooling. Mission education came under stringent criticism for attempting to raise the African to European standards, particularly in light of the emerging discourse of "culture" emanating from social anthropology. The Victorian idea of "civilizing" the native was replaced with a pseudoscientific discourse that argued for Africans to be educated in a manner that suited their abilities. Manzo (1992a) argues that this shift in discourse was a significant break as previously there was no necessary correlation between skin color and civilization. Anyone who became Christian would be viewed as civilized, and there was also the possibility that whites could be uncivilized. Now, however, the "science" of race provided for separate, biologically determined paths. Government-sponsored African education became synonymous with training for manual (boys) and domestic (girls) work. Furthermore, African education, under the 1922 Financial Relations Fourth Extension Act, was wholly financed through African taxation, thus severely limiting the available resources to be spent. Mission schools faced decreasing state subsidies, though they continued to educate significantly more

African children than the government schools (Horrell, 1963). At the same time, separate schooling for coloured and Indian children developed, establishing the rudimentary structures for the apartheid educational system that would soon follow.

BANTU EDUCATION AND THE CREATION OF RACIAL IDENTITIES

The National Party's victory in 1948 marked the beginning of the era of apartheid and the implementation of numerous legislative acts that defined everyday life in South Africa around one's racial classification. The Race Classification Act of 1950 (also known as the Population Registration Act) provided for the division of South Africans into specified racial groups, with each group accorded a particular location within a hierarchy—Afrikaners on the top, followed by other whites, Indians, coloureds, and Africans. [2] The Group Areas Act of 1950 (reformed in 1957) ensured that South Africans would live in racially demarcated and divided areas, and the Reservation of Separate Amenities Act, No. 49 (1953) guaranteed that public premises would be reserved for the exclusive use of one race only. These acts were forcibly implemented, with millions of individuals, predominantly black, required to relocate. Africans were made to leave "South Africa" and forced onto remote, barren, "ethnic" homelands (known as bantustans), which were governed by South African-appointed and controlled dictators. Men were allowed permits to reside in the cities so as to provide inexpensive labor for mines and other industry, and most often lived in crowded, filthy barracks, traveling home to see their families in the homelands once a year. Women and children, left without any means of support, and usually no electricity, running water, or other infrastructure, survived on the small amounts of money sent by their husbands and attempts to farm on the worst land in South Africa.

A system of stratified education was one of the key means through which the apartheid government attempted to maintain division and disparity. At its core, the apartheid educational system was designed to structure and reproduce inequality, by ensuring that blacks received an education that was grossly inferior to that provided to whites. One of the cornerstones of apartheid education, the Bantu Education Act of 1953, functioned on many levels—political, economic, social, and cultural—to contain blacks. For example, it has been argued that Bantu Education served the labor needs of the capitalist class (Kallaway, 1984; Unterhalter et al., 1991); that it was designed to create and reinforce ethnic identities among Africans, thus crushing emerging nationalist sentiments (Manzo, 1992a; Molteno, 1984) and that its aim was to eliminate the influence of missionary education (Dube, 1985). [3] Bantu Education cannot be considered one, monolithic, unchanging system of domination, but instead must be seen as a system that reformed itself philosophically as shifting political and economic conditions warranted (Unterhalter, 1991).

Bantu education required all schools, including those operated by churches and missions, to use a common syllabus. State subsidies for mission schools would also be eliminated over a four-year period, thus forcing the closure of many of these schools. Additionally, Bantu Education mandated that primary school education be conducted in the student's "mother tongue," thus recreating (and in many cases, creating) ethnic affiliations. The Bantu Education Act, followed by the Extension of University Education Act of 1959, Coloured Persons Education Act of 1963, the Indian Education Act of 1965, and the National Education Act of 1967 established the segregated and unequal system of mass schooling that, as Cross and Chisholm (1990) argue, became the basis for the construction of racial and ethnic subjects.

At the same time, however, race under apartheid was never an absolutely stable category; instead it was continually reformed. The apartheid government created and defined specific racial categories, invoking a mixture of scientific and new, or cultural, racism, to justify its policies. Manzo (1992) argues that the apartheid system was fueled not by a consistent application of population categorization, but by inconsistency, which was "an imperative, not an oversight" (p. 38). In other words, in order to maintain political and economic domination, the apartheid state had to deploy "race" in multiple and contradictory ways, which allowed for the maintenance and consolidation of white power and control. As an example, she cites the criteria used in the Population Registration Act (PRA), which provided for the classification of every individual. Manzo notes that though the act claimed to use "scientific" criteria to differentiate populations, in fact the PRA, "defined two of the races—White and Colored—by skin color; one—Native—by country of origin; and the fourth one—Asian—by continent of origin" (p. 37). Thus, the discourse of apartheid shifts gears as is necessary, invoking history, culture, nation, and biology to explain and perpetuate systems of domination. Rob Nixon (1994) also notes the inconsistencies in apartheid rhetoric and policies, as Africans are separated by defined criteria of language and culture, while whites with multiple lines of descent and languages (including Afrikaans, English, Portuguese, Greek, Hebrew, German, and Hungarian) constitute a single population group.

Dubow (1994, see also 1995) argues that "ethnicity" as an explanation for difference appeared in South Africa first in the 1930s and 1940s, as race as biology lost its explanatory power worldwide, and again in the 1960s and 1970s, as the apartheid government hijacked international movements for cultural pluralism and self-determination (including the multiple struggles for independence on the African continent) to justify its policy of separate development. Within the philosophy of Afrikaner nationalism, the separation of nations was also rhetorically premised on the lack of historical contact between whites and blacks, and the "empty land" thesis that proposed that whites had legitimate claims to South African territory because, they argue, the land was empty when the first European settlers arrived in the Cape. Racism, thus, was coded by appeals to the preservation of white national identity. Christian National Education, one of the philosophies underlying the South African educational system, was theoretically grounded in the development of these distinct "nations" under the broad rubric of Christianity. As a philosophy, Christian National Education (CNE), perhaps in marginally altered forms, was followed in many white schools, including Fernwood, well into the 1990s. [4]

CHALLENGES TO BANTU EDUCATION AND "RACE"

Bantu Education provided the framework for mass schooling of Africans, though it was never free, nor available to all. [5] School enrollments rose dramatically, more than doubling between 1953 and 1965, and doubling again between 1965 and 1975 (Untelhalter, 1991). Chisholm and Cross (1990) attribute dramatic growth in the early 1970s to shifts in state policy, which began to bend to industry needs for more educated workers and thus allowed increased enrollments in African schools, with only minimal increase in funding. Politically, the 1960s and early 1970s were a time of intense repression, with the banning of opposition parties in 1960, and the imprisonment of their leaders, including Nelson Mandela, in 1963.

Although Bantu Education had met with opposition from its inception (Lodge, 1984; Nkomo, 1990; Unterhalter et al., 1991), the introduction of Afrikaans as a language of instruction in 1976 led to small, limited boycotts that eventually grew into the landmark historical event known as the Soweto uprisings. With hundreds of children dead following the protests of June 1976, schools became a key site for political organizing and resistance. In 1979, the Congress of South African Students (COSAS) was established and school boycotts followed in the Cape (1980) and then more generally throughout the country in the mid-1980s. By this time, black schools throughout the country were in a permanent state of crisis, as resistance to the apartheid state surged. As apartheid as a system was challenged, "race" as a organizing concept was questioned and disputed. For example, the Azanian People's Organization (AZAPO) preached essential African identities, while the Black Consciousness Movement (BCM), led by Steve Biko, promulgated a "blackness" that included Africans, Indians, and coloureds (Biko, 1978). Under the umbrella of the African National Congress, Africans, Indians, and coloureds welcomed whites to join with them in promoting a philosophy of nonracialism. Nonracialism rejected the apartheid government's categorization of individuals by "race" and is thus in some tension with the current discourse of the "rainbow nation" that celebrates, not rejects, these differences (see Adam, 1995; Frederikse, 1990; and Price, 1997, on nonracialism and ethnic identity).

In the midst of this concerted, organized, and growing opposition, the state was sinking into an economic and political crisis. On the economic front, recession, an unstable gold price, falling profits, high inflation, and a shortage of skilled workers all contributed to the growing sense that the established apartheid system was unworkable. In response to this crisis of capitalism, the state instituted reforms that began a process of substituting the language of capitalism for the language of racial classification. This modernization of apartheid reflected the state's realization that some of its apartheid policies worked against the economic stability of the country (Levy, 1991; Nasson, 1990; Unterhalter, 1991; Wolpe, 1988). Politically, South Africa was no longer physically surrounded by supportive, white, colonialist regimes. Instead, as Angola (1975), Mozambique (1975), and Zimbabwe (1980) became independent, South Africa was increasingly isolated. In this environment, the state began to repackage apartheid under the guise of separate development, establishing and ideologically promoting the bantustans and giving the Indian and coloured education departments self-control. The government tried to split any developing coalitions between Africans and Indians/coloureds by establishing a Tricameral Parliament with Indian and coloured representation, and making small concessions to the African urban and bantustan middle class by providing increased and upgraded services, including access, for a tiny minority, to improved education.

THE OPEN SCHOOLS MOVEMENT: 1976–1986

Against this background of crisis and cursory reforms, the government was also attempting to improve its relations with other African countries. In 1973, the government approached selected white Catholic schools and requested that they admit the black children of African diplomats. However, similar privileges could not be granted to South African blacks. While the government's request to admit non-South African black children was accommodated, the schools that had admitted these children joined with other Catholic schools and began to meet with the government to negotiate for the admittance of local black children. Although the government denied these requests, some convent-administered schools defied the government and admitted black students. As desegregation of Catholic schools spread, philosophical issues about the implications of these changes became contested territory. Sr. Louis Michael addressed these issues in a statement prepared for the Catholic Department of Schools:

> Do we mean by integration the admission of a few numbers of other races into existing White schools, expecting them to conform to the way of life of the White pupil, to adopt his attitude and values? If we do, then we should think more deeply on this matter. (Christie, 1990, p. 23)

The philosophical differences over opening of white, Catholic schools should be contextualized within the political upheaval that characterized South African society in the 1970s. Because of the minute number of black students affected, the "opening" of white Catholic schools was of little concern to broader black political movements, who were occupied with ending the system of mass education which had denied opportunity to millions. Thus, the struggle over the terms of the integration of white, Catholic schooling would be fought primarily among white, religious leaders, who took differing political perspectives about the extent of reform necessary.

Ultimately, the more radically transformative view of integration was rejected, and the parameters of open schooling [6] became relatively defined and fixed as a reform movement that provided for limited access for black students, but no interrogation of church and societal structures. In 1986, the Private Schools Act officially brought the open schools under the jurisdiction of the white education department, though they were allowed to "render services" to other groups. However the impact of the Catholic open schools was relatively limited; by 1986 only 75 of these schools existed throughout the country, and the schools were still 79% white (South African Institute of Race Relations, 1989). Other private schools eventually followed the lead of the Catholic church and began to admit students of all races under a similar "open" philosophy.

Despite the perhaps symbolic importance of the open schools movement in challenging the state's hegemonic control of schooling, its impact was quite minor, affecting only a small percentage of children, and coexisting with apartheid policies as a troublesome, though limited and contained, exception.

THE OPENING OF WHITE STATE SCHOOLS

In the 1980s, the apartheid system was collapsing on multiple fronts, including education. Mass movements, such as the United Democratic Front (UDF) and the Congress of South African Trade Unions (COSATU) had irretrievably altered the political climate. The National Education Crisis Committee (NECC) was formed and called for the establishment of "people's education," a new system of education that would be democratic and nonracial (Kruss, 1988; Levin, 1991; Mashamba, 1990; Sisulu, 1986; Wolpe, 1991). Bantu Education, as a system designed to control the aspirations of Africans and school them for subservience, had failed. Instead South Africa was increasingly ungovernable and systemic change was immanent.

White government schools also faced a crossroads. Declining white populations, particularly in inner city and rural areas, threatened the closure of many white schools. Simultaneously, blacks were moving into these areas. For example, 60,000 blacks lived in central Johannesburg in 1989, but there were no provisions for education for them in these areas as the schools remained designated for whites only (Bot, 1990). By 1989, 26% of white school places were empty, while there was an acknowledged shortage of over 150,000 places in black schools (Christie, 1993). Although the initial opening of white, Catholic schools in the 1970s was only of peripheral concern to black groups because of the small numbers of black students involved, the empty seats and classrooms of white state schools in the late 1980s become symbolic of the inequality and absurdity of the apartheid system (Mncwabe, 1992, 1993). Opposition black-led groups rallied for black students to be allowed to fill empty places in white schools and some groups threatened to occupy empty white schools and use them to provide education to black students (South African Institute of Race Relations, 1990).

In 1990, South Africa began a transition to a new era, as the ANC and PAC (Pan African Congress) were unbanned and pillars of apartheid legislation, such as the Group Areas Act, were repealed. Although sweeping changes were announced in other areas, the government continually refused requests by numerous white schools to admit black pupils. However, in late 1990, the minister of white education, Piet Clase, announced a new model for limited school desegregation, which gave white schools the power to decide their own admission policies. It is important to note that these schools still continued to operate under their "own" affairs department, and that the legislation did not dissolve the racially based system of educational governance. In Clase's words, ". . .a change in the admission policy of the school may not detract from the traditional values and ethos of such school" (Christie, 1993, p.7). In what became known as the Clase Models, "Model A" permitted schools to become private but with reduced financial assistance from the state; "Model B" allowed schools to continue with the same level of funding, but gave them the right to adopt their own admission procedures; and "Model C" allowed for conversion to a semiprivate school. In all cases, schools had to comply with a 50% plus 1 white enrollment policy. In order to convert to one of these models, an elaborate voting process was imposed that gave decisionmaking power to white parents.

The Clase models were highly criticized from all quarters. The opening of white schools would have little impact on the masses of black students—they would still operate under the strictures of apartheid education and ultimately the change would barely affect equality of opportunity. Christie (1993) argues that in demographics and in philosophy, apartheid ideology would be maintained:

> Stipulations that schools would continue to operate within racially-based departments, that quotas would be monitored, and that the ethos of the schools would remain unaltered were evidence that the government was reformulating racial ideologies rather than abandoning them. (p. 9)

The apartheid government's moves towards the desegregation of white schools was similar to the position adopted by Catholic schools almost fifteen years earlier—allow a small number of black students into white schools, but permit no changes to the fundamental structure and ethos of the schools.

By the end of 1991, 667 of the 2,130 historically white schools had chosen Model B—most had voted for no change, and a handful had chosen other options (Christie, 1993). In effect, white parents had been given control over their own school's admission policy and most had chosen to remain segregated, even at the expense of perhaps losing their school to declining enrollment. By 1992, facing pressure to cut spending on white education, the new white minister of Education, Piet Marais, declared that all Model B schools would automatically be converted to Model C, unless they voted to retain Model B. Most schools, unable to once again rally parents for a complicated voting procedure, by default accepted Model C status, which decreased the school's state subsidy to 75%. A fourth option introduced by Marais, Model D, did allow white schools to operate without racial quotas. Only a handful of white schools throughout South Africa embraced this model.

Although the opening of white state schools received sustained media and public attention, Indian and coloured schools had been open to students of other racial classifications since 1985. By 1989, Indian schools enrolled 5,315 non-Indian students (Annual Report of the House of Delegates, 1989 in Carrim, 1992) and coloured schools enrolled 8,106 non-coloured (South African Institute of Race Relations, 1990). Furthermore, African schools under the jurisdiction of the Department of Education and Training (African schools outside of the homelands) enrolled over 4,000 coloured students in 1986 (Bot, 1990, p. 16). The reason for their enrollment, according to the DET's public relations department, is that

> during a transition phase in the fifties and sixties, a very small percentage of brown pupils attended schools for blacks and vice versa. This was done, and is still done, in accordance with practical guidelines mutually agreed upon by the two departments mainly with regard to the availability of facilities and always serving the best interests of the child, (Bot, 1990, p. 16)

Although the numbers of students enrolled in schools different from their legal population classification was clearly quite small [7] I note the phenomenon for two reasons: 1) despite apartheid philosophies, education departments serving African, coloured, and Indian students were, it appears, less rigid than white education departments about issues of desegregation in schools and 2) absolute segregation was never a complete and total state of affairs, though exceptions were isolated.

From the perspective of the government, the opening of white schools was a response to a changing political and economic situation, not a fundamental shift in ideology. White schools, for the most part, followed the government's position: opening the schools to children of all races, without questioning the underlying ideologies and philosophies.

THE EXPERIENCE OF MULTIRACIAL SCHOOLING

Before the 1990s, only limited research on multiracial schooling existed, most notably Christie's (1990) scholarship on open Catholic schools in the 1980s. But as multiracial schooling became the norm at white government schools throughout the country, there was increased interest in the experiences of the students, teachers, administrators, and parents who were seen as the harbingers of the South Africa to come.

During the apartheid years, nonracialism was a guiding principle of the opposition movement (primarily the African National Congress and affiliated United Democratic Front). Seeking to reject apartheid's systemic segregation, proponents of nonracialism struggled to reject "race" as a category of identification, while at

the same time recognize that race's significance in a still-stratified society could
not be ignored.

One of the most important aspects of this early research on desegregated
schools is its focus on how white administrators and teachers (and students in
Christie's study) responded to the arrival of black children. Unlike Fernwood in
1996 (where black children are in the majority), these studies examine the more
common situation in the 1990s, where black children constitute substantially less
than half (often only one-third) of the student population. By the 1990s, many
multiracial schools prided themselves on what one principal described as "a race-
free school" (Penny et al., 1993, p. 424). Another principal interviewed by Penny
et al. was "adamant that once an African enters the school gates the boy becomes
simply another student, one whose racial background is irrelevant to all concerned" (p. 426). Nonracialism in these cases translates into a denial of race and
becomes part of the larger trend towards assimilation and stasis, instead of change
and transformation. With the numbers of black students in these schools still aver-
aging 25 to 33% (and the vast majority of these students middle class), there is
little pressing need to reexamine institutional structures and priorities.

Teachers and administrators often insist that nothing about the school
has changed. Instead, blacks simply adjust to the already constituted ethos of
the school. One teacher in Crain Soudien's (1994) study remarked:

> I think blacks in this school still respect the traditions and they really under-
> stand that it is a good school and that they must try to fit in and respect the
> school. So I think that they don't have to really adjust, they just come to the
> school. (p. 285)

Christie (1990) argues that in their refusal to support integration open schools
were instead choosing to adopt an assimilationist philosophy:

> In their institutional dimensions—premises, staffing, curriculum, sporting and
> other extramural activities—most open schools carry a powerful legacy of
> white education . . . the established assumptions of white schooling have acted
> as gatekeepers against fundamental change, and have provided the material
> conditions for assimilationism. (p. 192)

Contradictorily, these newly admitted black children are seen as both special and different from other blacks, and simultaneously as inferior. Many schools
took comfort in denying the "blackness" of their black students, instead emphasizing their familiarity with and acceptance of white norms. Referring to the home
life of an African student in his school, one headmaster commented:

> Alan Khumalo's father is an insurance broker, his mother is a teacher. Their
> home language at this stage is English and they stay in a mansion . . . . I don't
> think you can compare Alan to the next guy who has grown up on the farm,
> who can't speak English. (Sadie, 1993, p. 108)

Similarly, a teacher in David Sadie's study separated "her" black children from her imaginings of authentic black life in South Africa: "When we went on tour to Natal we went to Zululand. We went to a traditional Zulu kraal and some of the black children were horrified that there was no television and life was so completely different from what they knew" (p. 142). This teacher justified the presence of black children in her school by separating them from rural blackness, which she read as authentic, though it is quite likely that the Zulu kraal they visited was a re-creation and re-presentation of an imagined Zuluness designed to entertain tourists (Golan, 1994; Nixon, 1994). Nevertheless, the teacher accepted this re-creation as the definition of blackness and noted with relief that her students were civilized enough to appreciate television.

At the same time, however, black children were also constructed as inferior, so as not to threaten the balance of power and privilege within society. A teacher at an Indian school (Carrim, 1992) explains her reaction to the academic success of African children, "I am always surprised when a black child does well because I don't expect them to. That's how I realised I am prejudiced as well. I am trying to confront it now "(p. 21). A white student in Christie's (1990) study similarly comments, "...the general thing about it is that they are lower than us. You know what I mean, like it's just people. I don't know. They are, and that's why they get lower pay than a white man" (p. 74).

The inferiority of blacks is constantly re-encoded through concern about the lowering of academic and behavioral standards when they are admitted to formerly all-white schools. For example, one of Penny et al.'s (1993) major findings is that principals were concerned with bringing African students "up to standard" and "whether standards would be maintained" (p. 416). Black children were also blamed for being loud and disruptive. One teacher in Sadie's study (1993) observed, "The black children are very different to the white children in their culture and everything and especially in the noise level. The noise level immediately shot up" (p. 137).

Far from being models for a newly democratic nation, the majority of multiracial schools in the 1990s retained the values and practices of earlier years, while allowing a small, contained, select number of black students to join their communities, if only on the periphery.

THIS STUDY IN CONTEXT

The research on the lived experience of schooling in South Africa, both past and present, is quite limited. As Soudien (1996) observes, schooling under apartheid was a "black box," as "the apartheid authorities made schools off-limits to all but the most politically submissive" (p. 11). These restrictions, and the political climate under apartheid, severely limited the possibilities for substantial earlier research that may have probed the questions of identity and race that are central to this study. Two of the most significant exceptions are the work of Soudien (1996,

1998) who specifically investigates the impact of the apartheid school on African and coloured students' production of identities, and Christie (1990) who focuses her study on the experiences of students (as opposed to administrators or teachers) at multiracial Catholic schools in the 1980s.

As political change comes to South Africa, the amount of research in schools will increase, and there will more studies that, like this one, use ethnographic methods to investigate educational, sociological, and cultural questions. [8] Clearly, the experiences of youth (both in and outside of school) in the immediate post-apartheid era is an area of research that demands further development. Methodologically, all the cited studies employ qualitative, though not extended ethnographic, methods. Thus my study of Fernwood expands and deepens this literature, as I weave interview data with ethnographic examples gathered over the course of one year.

Throughout this book, I argue that to analyze Fernwood youths' construction of racialized identities, it is necessary to interrogate their relationship to global flows. At the same time, South Africa is clearly saturated with its own history: of apartheid, of a (relatively) peaceful and rapid transition to democracy, and of the current struggle for a decent and humane existence for all of its people. That history provided the circumstance that made this study possible, and serves as a frame within which the study rests. Yet, South Africa is only a click away from the United States, Britain, Europe, Australia, Canada, and anywhere else on the globe. Its reality, and its youth's engagement with race and popular culture, may be formative not only of its own future, but of many others'.

CHAPTER THREE

DAILY LIFE AT FERNWOOD

L ocated in a valley in a quiet, lower-middle-class white neighborhood next to a park, Fernwood, in the 1980s, could easily have felt as isolated as a school in a small, rural town. In 1985, a typical year, Fernwood's rugby team lost twelve games out of sixteen, the school play was *Boeing, Boeing*, the boys' cadets program became an integrated part of the school curriculum, and the school's first computers arrived. In this year, its twentieth anniversary, Fernwood's students and staff are still virtually all white. The only blacks on the premises except one (a biology laboratory assistant) were cleaning and maintenance staff. Despite the boycotts, states of emergency, and general crisis enveloping South African society, life at Fernwood was remarkably normal, full of field trips, cricket games, and dances. In this aspect, Fernwood was representative of many white communities and schools that continued to deny that tinkering at apartheid's edges was inadequate, and had little idea of the future that awaited them.

Like other white schools, Fernwood was a product of apartheid South Africa, and the specific context of Durban. Durban, a port city of four million people located on the Indian Ocean, was deliberately partitioned under apartheid, dividing white Durban from Indian, coloured, and African areas. Durban's extent of racial segregation was so extreme that Paul Maylam (1985) refers to the city as a "pioneer in the establishment of urban segregation in South Africa" (p. 47). Durban created this whiteness through the forced removal of Africans, Indians, and coloureds from more central locations in the city to outlying townships, and, in the case of Africans, to townships officially located in the bantustan of KwaZulu. By the 1990s, however, violence and lack of job opportunities in the African areas had driven many people into informal settlements in the Durban metropolitan area. Doug Hindson and Jeff McCarthy (1994), drawing on studies conducted by the Urban Foundation, estimate that in 1992 26% (almost all Africans) of KwaZulu Natal's population lived in informal settlements, for the most part without running water, electricity, sanitation, or permanent employment.

The vast majority of Indian South Africans (almost one million) reside in the Durban metropolitan area. Most of these Indians are descendants of 150,000 indentured workers brought from India to work on the Natal sugar plantations from 1860 to 1911 (Freund, 1995). A dramatically smaller number came voluntarily and established themselves as traders. Threatened by the financial success of a small number of Indians, strong anti-Indian feelings erupted among Durban's white community who attempted to segregate Indians, restrict their economic activity and land tenure, and called for their repatriation to India. Before, during, and after the apartheid years tensions exist between Indians and all other racial groups including coloureds. Cliffie Collings, a founder of an anti-apartheid organization in Natal's coloured community during the 1980s, explains some of these strains:

> Now the problem would be that the coloureds are exposed only to the Indians who own the businesses in Grey Street [a main commercial area in Durban], or Indians who come to their discos all flashy. They're not exposed to people deep within, say, Phoenix or Chatsworth [outlying Indian townships], to some of the Indians who are suffering. They pick up anti-Indian vibes, you can see it all the time.... (Frederickse, 1990, pp. 192–193)

Because of the sizable Indian population and numerically tiny coloured population, Durban's demographics differ significantly from other parts of South Africa. In 1996, the total population of KwaZulu-Natal, of which Durban is the largest city, was 8,417,021. Of this number, 6,880,652 (81.7%) were African; 790,813 (9.4%) were Indian; 558,182 (6.6%) were white; 117,951 (1.4%) were coloured; and 69,423 (.8%) were unspecified or other. [1] Although coloureds constitute a numerical majority in the Western Cape, for example, their presence in Durban is quite small. The same picture, in reverse, holds for Indians. It is also noteworthy that the majority of whites in Durban are descendants of English, not Afrikaner, settlers. Thus, while the politics of Afrikaans, both as a language and a point of cultural contestation, may be significant in areas such as Cape Town or the Orange Free State, such issues have little impact in Durban. Similarly, while debates over the relationship between Afrikaans and the coloured community may be prevalent in Cape Town (Owen, 1996), most coloureds in Durban are more comfortable with English. The particular dynamics of Durban, with its population demographics, must be considered when comparing Durban to other parts of South Africa or generalizing from Durban to the whole country.

FERNWOOD IN TRANSITION

Founded in 1965, Fernwood was an all-boys' school until 1976, when, due to low enrollments, girls were admitted. By becoming coed, Fernwood was unique among white schools in Durban. Even in 1996, there was only one other coed white (Model C) school in the metropolitan area, a technical high school that began to admit a small number of girls in the 1990s. Throughout its history, Fernwood has been unable to compete with the more prestigious white schools in Durban. Gene du Plessis, who has taught at Fernwood since 1983, describes the school as an "orphan" school, which has consistently failed to attract the best students—or teachers. However, its small size promoted a feeling of cohesiveness among students and staff, which is rare in a South African high school. As Mr. du Plessis reflects:

> We've been surrounded by big schools, Glenmore Girls High School, South-
> wood, and they creamed off all the quality, and we were left with whatever hap-
> pened to be left. Nevertheless, although we didn't have the same quality as the
> other schools, it was always a very small school. At that time we had only 380
> pupils in the entire school; it was a tiny school. In fact we were threatened quite
> often with being closed down because we were not a viable proposition.
> And the staff was never ideal, it's not the sort of school which ever encour-
> aged large numbers of really tremendous teachers. But I think the staff and
> the pupils, because of the small numbers, knew one another so intimately,
> there really was a sense of family about that place. And when I first got here,
> it reminded me of some tiny little town out there in the boondocks, where
> everybody knew everybody else, and it had its own sort of charm about it.

Fernwood's story of transition began in 1990. Fernwood, like other white government schools, would have to vote, either for change or against it. Given Fernwood's history of below-average enrollment and its second-rate reputation, it seemed
inevitable that, whether voluntary or not, Fernwood would eventually be compelled
to fill its open spaces with black pupils or face closure. At Fernwood's annual prizegiving day in 1990, shortly before the vote, the then headmaster, Thomas Venter,
urged parents to vote for change. As the 1990 yearbook reports, he advised, ". . . it
would be far better for us to make the decisions and establish the conditions now than
to be compelled to open the school to all, without conditions, in the near future."
The Chair of the Fernwood Governing Board in 1996, Linda Joubert, concurred that
for many white schools, the initial decision to admit black students was made with
the intention of being able to select and control those who would be admitted:

> I sat in many a meeting, not necessarily Fernwood, where in actual fact a num-
> ber of white parents said if we go Model B, we've got control and we just up
> the school fees and we will only take the nice blacks.

Ninety percent of Fernwood parents voted; of that number, 86% voted for change.
Model B status (which was quickly converted to Model C by the government)

conferred on Fernwood the ability to set its own fees and admission regulations
and to admit black students, as long as white students remained in the majority.

The initial years of integration at Fernwood were relatively easy: black (predominantly African) students who were admitted were academically and athlet-
ically talented and dedicated to involvement in the school community. Many of
the black students rose to positions of leadership and influence in the school, and
Fernwood's emerging identity as the "new South Africa" school gave it a sense of
pride and achievement that was an uncommon experience for a school that had
always struggled. Teachers were proud of the black students who arrived at Fernwood. Mr. du Plessis recollects that

> when we had that first bunch, they used to be so successful at athletics, our
> athletics was actually blossoming and the black pupils were part of that, and
> they were successful. They were winning in Durban and districts. And the
> other black pupils saw them being successful, and they thought this is some-
> thing to aspire to.

The black students excelled in other areas as well. Anne Potts, a Fernwood teacher
from 1988, remembered that the initial intake of black students were hard workers, and "clever kids from good backgrounds," as compared to the current students,
which she describes as more "riff-raff."

Pleased with its initial success, Fernwood, unlike other Model C schools,
allowed its black student population to grow rapidly. Warren Korte, a geography
teacher, proudly recalls:

> [Fernwood's] at the forefront of change in South Africa; we were the first
> school to become a Model B school, to admit black pupils. We didn't just
> admit them, we admitted them in large numbers, which as a result we are
> quick to change.

Academic results at the school were also up slightly in 1991, with a matric (senior year) exam pass rate of 92%, a few percentage points above recent years.

By early 1993, Fernwood was featured in a news report in the leading Durban
daily newspaper as the most racially integrated school in the area, with a 1993 population of almost 30% black students. Throughout this year, pictures of black and
white Fernwood students appeared frequently in local newspapers, as Fernwood
aggressively promoted its image as a multiracial school oriented towards change.
Fernwood was slowly becoming recognized as a pioneering school, as Mr. Venter
reported at prizegiving day: "As leaders in the multi-cultural experiment, we presented a seminar at the school on Multi-cultural Education which was extremely well
received by the academic community in Natal." Towards the end of 1993, Fernwood
purchased a full page in a supplement section of the leading Sunday newspaper in
Durban, which promoted the school, particularly its multicultural character. The page
featured quotes from parents, teachers, staff, pupils, and the administration lauding
Fernwood's achievements, its position as the most racially integrated school in

Durban, and its unique ability to prepare students for the new South Africa, highlighted in its slogan, "Fernwood: Preparing for a new generation."

In 1994, the school's black population shot up to 40%, and it continued to climb: by 1996, two-thirds of the school was black. As the numbers of black students increased, suddenly the school became less concerned about its image as a new South Africa school and more worried about its declining white enrollment and the large number of poorer black students who were enrolling. Bridging classes were eliminated because of complaints from black parents of segregation, compounded by budget problems, and the new black students were not as easily assimilated into the school. Increasingly poorer, these black students experienced greater hardships than their middle-class predecessors. Clayton van Zyl, an Afrikaans teacher, remembers the difficulties the school encountered as it struggled to cope with its changing black population:

> The blacks had different problems to ours, and there was a mindset we didn't understand. Teachers didn't understand why they didn't do their homework, and they [the teachers] had to learn about having no electricity, and taking a long time with transport on the buses, and the strikes that make it hard to come to school.

Although Fernwood was still administering admission tests to black students (except for those from Model C primary schools), it nonetheless found itself admitting more black pupils and slowly losing whites. As both Michael Green and Jeanne Deacon, deputy vice-principals, confirmed, Fernwood began accepting white students who had been expelled from other schools just to maintain racial balance. In contrast, academically qualified black students languished on a waiting list that in 1996 numbered 200. The administration justified this policy on the basis that black parents wanted their children to go to school with whites so they would learn English. The white population of the school, always lower middle and working class, was also becoming poorer, as wealthier and more academically talented students found that they could suddenly enter the more prestigious schools in Durban; schools that, under the apartheid system, would not have admitted them. However, the outflow of whites (both out of South Africa and to private schools) had created spaces in these more prestigious schools that were desperate to keep their student bodies overwhelmingly white. Fernwood, at the bottom of white Durban schools, became a mix: older middle-class black students who entered Fernwood in the early 1990s; working-class and poor black students from the mid-1990s, and working-class and poor white students who, despite the changes, still could not get into the more exclusive white schools. As Terry Pieters, a department head, remarks, "This school has become a "reject" school—every parent thinks it's just their kid that is here because he couldn't get into a better school, but it's almost everyone."

In five years, Fernwood's black population had increased sixfold; what had begun as a bold experiment in integration, widely lauded by the media and the

local community, had become a school laden with conflicts, problems, and racial
tensions. Many of the teachers and administrators at the school blamed the former headmaster, Mr. Venter (who retired in 1995), for opening the school too
quickly, without proper thought and procedures for implementation of the large-
scale change. But for Fernwood, at the bottom of the hierarchy of white schools
in Durban, change could not be avoided.

FERNWOOD HIGH IN 1996

As 1996 begins at Fernwood High School, its coed student population of 600
is approximately 66% black (including a small number of coloured and Indian
pupils) and 33% white. During this year, I collected data on race, racial identity, and change in South Africa through an ethnographic case study of Fernwood High. My role at the school was loosely defined: I attended classes, school
events, and extracurricular activities, spent time with students before, during,
and after school, and on the weekends and school holidays. I also spent a considerable amount of time with teachers, administrators, and the school's governing board: attending meetings, school functions, and informal gatherings.
As my study focused on the racial identities of older students (predominantly
grade 12), this book primarily represents their experiences. However, I also
spent time with, and interviewed, students at all grade levels. In total, I conducted interviews about race, racial identity, and change at Fernwood and in
South Africa with over 100 students (of all races present in the school and both
genders) both individually and in groups, the majority (twenty three) of the
teaching and management staff, and a small number of parents and governing
board members. Additionally, fifty three students in two English classes (grade
11 and 12) wrote essays on their racial, ethnic, and national identities. (See
the appendix for a full discussion of methodology.)

As is typical at most newly desegregated formerly white schools in 1996,
Fernwood's teaching and management staff is almost exclusively white. Of
twenty nine teachers and administrators at Fernwood, only three are not white,
all teachers: one African (the Zulu language teacher), one coloured, and one
Indian. The management, which consists of the headmaster, three deputy vice-
principals, and two department heads, is completely white and, with one exception (Jeanne Deacon, a deputy vice-principal), all male. Although there are an
increasing number of African graduates from formerly white universities
and teacher training programs, none has yet been hired at Fernwood. Jeanne
Deacon explains the challenge:

> a lot of the blacks [Africans] have a three-year training college diploma,
> whereas most of the Indians, coloureds, and whites have four years or a var-
> sity degree and a year. So they tend to take those on certain grounds of bet-
> ter qualifications. So there's still that gap that's got to be filled.

In contrast to the homogeneity of the teaching staff, students pour into Fernwood from all corners of Durban: some walk to school from nearby neighborhoods, others travel two or more hours on buses, trains, and their feet. Most of
them bring with them the experiences of growing up in segregated areas: some
the exclusive segregation of white suburbs, others the imposed and desperate
poverty of the townships. African students at Fernwood do not share a uniform
class background; some are wealthy, living in palatial homes in formerly white
suburbs (or more affluent sections of the townships), others cannot even afford
one properly fitted school uniform. In the older grades, particularly among the
matriculants (grade 12), the majority of African students are from middle-class
or working-class homes. The sons and daughters of teachers, nurses, and other
professionals, these students were part of the first wave of African children to
attend white government schools in the early 1990s. Some attended multiracial
Catholic schools in the 1980s, others the few academically oriented and com-
petitive black schools. Their families tend to live in the formerly white suburbs
near the school, although many students still return to the African townships
every weekend. Numbuso explains that she finds the white suburbs "too dead for
me," and goes back to the township as much as possible:

> Every weekend I go to Zena's place or Thandeka's place or wherever, every
> weekend I go to the township, because I cannot live without people. In the
> white areas, there aren't any blacks. There's a little bit of them, a minority of
> them. So people, like you know, they're not nice. I don't think they're nice.

However, a substantial number of African students, predominantly in the lower
grades, are from poor and working poor households. Many of these students only
transferred to white schools in their high school years, having received their early
schooling in township schools. Less privileged and less academically prepared, they
struggle with English and with the vast gulf that separates Fernwood from everything they had known before.

The white students at Fernwood, fewer in number, are also poorer and less
academically able than their predecessors. Included among the white students at
Fernwood are some of the poorest whites in the Durban area. Some of the white
boys are orphans who live in group homes and institutions; others are from poor
or working class families. A teacher tells me about two white children, brother
and sister, who must alternate sleeping outside in a tent because there is inadequate sleeping space in the house. Not all whites at Fernwood are poor—particularly among the matriculants there are a substantial number of white students from
middle-class and working-class homes generally located in the immediate area.
But the trend at Fernwood is clear, as younger students, both African and white,
are poorer, more troubled, and less academically prepared than their predecessors.

Fernwood's coloured and Indian student population is small. Many of the
older coloured students (about 10% of the matriculants) came to Fernwood because
of teacher strikes in coloured schools. Economically, many are from working-class

homes, equal to or, in some cases, less privileged, than their African peers. Like their African counterparts, the older coloured students travel long distances from outlying coloured townships to attend Fernwood. Younger coloured students are more likely to be from families that have left the coloured townships to settle in the immediate area surrounding Fernwood. Many of these students are at Fernwood only at their parents' insistence. Despite the distances they would need to travel, these students would prefer to attend the coloured schools; they feel alienated and unconnected both at Fernwood and in their new, middle-class, predominantly white, neighborhoods. While the socioeconomic status of Africans and whites drops noticeably through the grade levels, the coloured student population of Fernwood reverses this trend, as the school now draws its coloured students primarily from the surrounding middle-class neighborhoods.

Indian students constitute only a handful of Fernwood students, primarily because of the historic racism of Durban's whites towards Indians, and thus Indians' well-founded mistrust of white schools. The few Indian students at Fernwood tend to associate themselves most closely with the coloured students, an alliance that exemplifies the paradoxical relationship between Indians and coloureds in Durban. Despite the tensions noted earlier in the chapter, there are also a significant numbers of marriages, and thus family ties, between coloureds and Indians. Charles, a coloured student, tries to balance these two realities:

> the coloureds generally feel Indians look down on them. I don't think it's true, but you can just feel it. If you go into a coloured area and you are Indian, you can just feel everybody doesn't want you there. You get that feeling; same way if a coloured goes into an Indian area. My dad's sister is married to an Indian guy. We invite him for supper, he'll come and sit outside in the car or something. They just don't feel comfortable in our presence. It's just the way it is.

Unsure of each other, but even more suspicious of whites and Africans, Indian and coloured students form slender bonds.

ZONE OF COLLISION

The year 1996 begins and ends in relative disorder and confusion. As the black, specifically African, student population has grown over the past few years, the celebratory discourses of the "new South Africa" and the "rainbow nation" school have disappeared. Instead, the school is overwhelmed by disciplinary and academic problems. Few teachers or administrators will deny that the school has problems: Most explain them as rooted in cultural differences between a majority African student population and an almost completely white staff. A first-year teacher, Debbie Ingram, summarizes her early experiences at Fernwood as "culture shock," and finds herself differing with her pupils on things such as coming on time to class, study habits, and keeping quiet when others are talking. She notes that "they yell and scream and carry on, it's not in their nature to be quiet. It's hard to cope with because I don't want to make them feel that they can't be themselves." Others blame the students' poverty, poor academic background, and apartheid. For example, Terry Pieters is disillusioned because he used to believe that

> if you just took the kids out of the township environment, and provided them with a decent education, then everything would come right. But in fact what's happened is that the kids have brought the township with them. Kids don't work, there are no standards, and there are language difficulties.

Throughout the year students and teachers clash on a regular and increasing basis. From many teachers' perspectives, students are noisy, disruptive, uncooperative, and lazy. A first-year teacher, Justin Bishop, describes his major function as "riot control," and relates that during his first week at the school students in his registration class were "cutting each other's hair off, setting fire to desks, and pissing in lunchboxes."

Even more experienced teachers are overwhelmed by the daily chaos of the school, the changing policies and priorities of the management, and the increasing sense that the management cannot control the school nor will they consider substantive change. As Warren Korte, who has taught at Fernwood for five years, grimly observes,

> I'm in survival mode. You speak to most of the teachers you're in survival mode. You walk around with huge blinkers. You just don't see things purposely. Because if you start doing things you are going to land with so much follow-up that you're going to drown yourself.

Teachers, administrators, and governing board members generally perceive that the quality of students has deteriorated and that the school is battling to maintain control. Linda Joubert, the Chair of the governing board, recognizes that Fernwood is in the midst of a crisis:

> I think they're teaching blind at the moment; they're praying and spraying. They'll try anything to get something to work, but I don't think they've got it. They're really at the bottom of their resources in terms of knowing how to get there.

Over the past few years Fernwood has responded to some of the specific concerns and problems of its now majority black population. For example, the school day in 1996 starts at 7:50 A.M., later than in previous years to allow students adequate time for travel from outlying townships. The school also established a study period in 1996: The last period of each day is now devoted to doing homework and studying to compensate for many students' lack of time and space for studying at home. This new practice is only partially successful and by the middle of the year the study period has become an extra lesson period for the matriculants and a testing period, on many days, for other students. Despite these changes, problems persist and in some areas increase as the year goes on.

STUDENT'S LIVES: EXPERIENCING FERNWOOD

Fernwood in 1996 did nothing to mediate or facilitate the strained relations among students. This position of inaction is in marked contrast to some Model C schools, which had developed, or were developing, programs designed to address the conflicts and strains experienced by multiracial, economically mixed student bodies. Charmaine, a coloured student, explains the difference between her previous school, a Model C girls' school, and Fernwood:

> At Lakewood Girls' if you said anything racist, you were sent to the headmistress. At this school, we say racist things all the time, and nothing happens to you. The point is you can't hide racism, so you might as well just be open and get it over with.

Unlike the majority of Model C schools in Durban, Fernwood lacks even the veneer of tolerance, equality, and respect. Instead, as Charmaine suggests, blatant racism is allowed to flourish, creating a situation in which attempts at dialogue, understanding, and cooperation are few. Consequently, black students often relate experiences of racism and marginalization within the school. While black students everywhere have certainly faced racism in majority white schools (i.e., in South Africa—see Christie, 1990; in Great Britain—see Troyna & Hatcher, 1992), black Fernwood students in a majority-black school still feel discrimination, both within the microdynamics of small pockets of the school where whites are numerically superior (i.e., the rugby team), and more generally. Simphiwe writes about his involvement on the school rugby team:

> I feel more comfortable when I am with my race than when I am with other races. I discovered this two years ago when I played rugby in one of the school's teams. In my team I was the only black player. I did not feel comfortable in the team because I was not able to express myself in English properly. Besides that we had lots of differences . . . .One of the things that I did not like in the team was that sometimes teammates were talking about me as if I was not there or as if I did not understand what they were saying. Sometimes they were calling me in any Zulu name and that drove me mad.

Another African boy, Molefe, recognizes the extra effort he must put forward to succeed in Fernwood's environment:

> For me as a black person to come to this school I have to work more, to go that extra mile. I have to prove myself, even in sports; everything I do I have to go that extra mile. I have to justify myself, more than a person of another race. Because there will always be that race thing in other people's eyes.

Finally, Tanya, a coloured girl, relates an encounter with a white boy that she interprets as racial:

> I've experienced many racial differences in this school. Like one was over a month ago, I was standing on the stairs, and this white boy he's spitting on the stairs . . . this green ooze is coming out of his mouth, and I found that extremely disgusting. And I just stood there looking up at him, and he said, "Do you want me to spit on you?" I said, "Why don't you come and try it?" So he actually spat on me, so I went to the top [of the stairs] and I said, "What the hell did you do that for," and he said, "Oh," and he pushed me. So I pushed him back; because he's stronger than me I was going to hit him back. Then Ms. Randele came outside, and she made me take all the blame for that.

Tanya's story highlights the recurring, low-level hostility that simmers, and occasionally erupts, between students of different races. Racially motivated, public fights occur several times during the year. More frequent, less noted, and less visible are the small everyday aggravations of the incident Tanya recalls, racial taunting, tripping students of other races as they walk down a corridor or a classroom aisle, and throwing items at other students' heads. All these behaviors, unchallenged by the administration, define, more than academics or the space of the classroom, many Fernwood students' experiences in school.

Despite this atmosphere, a substantial proportion of the black students I interviewed, and interacted with every day, did not feel that they experienced racism at Fernwood. For example, many African and coloured students were more concerned with the increased rules and discipline that they encounter at Fernwood than the racism of their classmates or teachers. Melissa, a coloured girl, comments on the difference between the coloured school in her area and Fernwood:

> My mother tells me about the people in the coloured school there, she leaves for work at half past seven, and school starts at 8 o'clock. People aren't even to school at 8 o'clock, they are still walking to school. We would already be in class at 8 o'clock, and they're still taking their time going to school, walking.

Sina, another coloured student, complains about what she sees as the nonsensical and random rules at Fernwood:

> stupid rules like that you have to wear a blazer. Go to a coloured school, they don't have to wear a blazer . . . . They [the administration and teachers] are so strict and hard, but like now, the main reason that I am going to stay, that I am not going to ask my mother again [to change schools] is because of my friends. I feel at home here. Even though it's a terrible place, it's a hell hole, I kind of like it.

For some black students, the administration's constant emphasis on sports (to be discussed in chapter 4) is a continual nuisance, particularly for girls like Debra, an African student, who are concerned about traveling home in the dark:

I think it's a waste of time. It would be better if I lived near. When I played
sport after school, and go home at half-past four, I have to get changed, shower,
and catch maybe a train at 6 o'clock, and it's not safe anymore.

Although it could certainly be argued that the administration's callous attitude
towards students' safety is racially based, Debra does not interpret their actions in
this paradigm, and instead reluctantly accepts this integral facet of school life.

Despite the strictness of the school and complaints about sports, black students
stay because of their friends, and critically because either they and/or their parents
recognize the substantial future benefits of the value of a matric certificate (a high
school diploma) from Fernwood instead of a black school. Over the course of the
year, few students leave Fernwood voluntarily. Black students (and their parents) who
recognize and experience racism at Fernwood make decisions to tolerate the situation because of the value of the degree. Others do not recognize racism as an important factor in their experience at Fernwood—despite any difficulties they may
encounter, Fernwood is still substantially better than the township schools. Thabo
discusses the realities of life in the majority of African schools in the townships:

> My mother didn't want us to go and study in black schools because they did-
> n't have facilities, all the windows are broken, and in the winter when it rains
> it's always cold, the rain will come inside the class, and you have to share the
> desks. She just didn't like us to get involved in the township, or like, nearby
> where I stayed, small boys smoke and all those things. And she didn't want
> me to adopt those kind of habits, and then she sent me away.

Purity, another African student, comments on the differences in teacher–student
interaction between Fernwood and her previous school:

> The education, I mean, the system of teaching in black schools is com-
> pletely different from white. It's much easier here, because the teacher is
> not pushing, he asks whether the people understand. You know in black
> schools, he or she gets upset because he's teaching a huge number of peo-
> ple and they make a noise and stuff. If you don't understand it's your busi-
> ness, you have no one to turn to discuss your problems if you've got prob-
> lems at home.

As Purity's quote reflects, black students at Fernwood are caught between feeling marginalized and excluded at a school most would characterize as white, and simultaneously asserting that Fernwood teachers show them greater care and concern than the
teachers at their previous schools. This ambivalence highlights a peculiar, contradictory reality that existed for black students at Fernwood and perhaps other Model
C schools in South Africa in the mid 1990s: Apartheid's legacy had led to a situation
in which students were both better educated and happier in a conflict-ridden school
with deep racial divides than in a black school that was struggling to survive.

While black students experience Fernwood as newcomers and outsiders, the
dwindling numbers of white students at Fernwood often express the feeling that

"their" school has been invaded, and that black students are privileged, both within school and out. As Sandy writes,

> A few years ago living in a white body was bearable, but now it's regrettable. Before I was born the black people were treated badly, now that their race president is in charge they have taken over and they want their revenge, it's just unfortunate that it's the white people of today that have to suffer . . . . I feel I'm crammed in a little box and until I paint my skin black and I act like a black person I'm not coming out!

In revealing these frustrations, and in Sandy's case the extreme of wanting to "paint my skin black," white students express that they now feel like victims. Jackie, another white student, feels that her school, and the sanctity of her lunch period, has been destroyed by the presence of African students:

> I think it's the volume level. It's the way they act, it's the way they can just stand in the middle of the field and start singing, and you'll be trying to enjoy a quiet lunch with your friends, and all of a sudden you have frigging girls choir in the middle of the field. That can get a bit irritating, because we don't do stuff like that. So it's like we don't do it, so why do you?

Jackie's question remained unanswered. Collisions over difference, anchored in over 400 years of colonialism, imperialism, and apartheid, flourish, as Fernwood is unwilling and unable to embrace the totality of its new world.

"THE GRAVEYARD OF EVERY GOOD TEACHER"

As the school becomes progressively unmanageable and laden with racial tensions, the administration responds in contradictory ways: It imposes itself more on students, becoming stricter, harsher, and more concerned with discipline, and when that fails shifts responsibility for student behavior to the individual classroom teachers. Teachers fall into several blocs. Many older teachers align themselves with the management, dismissing the (African) students as "animals" and bemoaning the general state of the school, its standards, and South African society; a substantial number of younger teachers join the South African Democratic Teachers Union (SADTU), and focus their energy on quietly building support to challenge the management's undemocratic practices. A third bloc of teachers try to sidestep the increasing tension between the management and SADTU members, instead working diligently both inside and outside the classroom to help individual students. Finally, a few teachers pay little attention to the politics of the school or the deteriorating quality of daily life. They frequently call in sick and do the minimum required when they do come to school.

Forces outside the school also contribute to the instability of day-to-day life inside. Because of shifts in the educational structure at the provincial level, many members of the school's management, as at all Model C schools in KwaZulu-Natal, are formally in acting posts. Model C schools are slated to be dissolved the following year and all hiring is now coordinated through a central provincial system, replacing the former racially based administrative structures. For example, an active search for a new headmaster of Fernwood for 1997 is under way throughout 1996.

In addition to the reality that the management of the school will change in the near future, the composition of the teaching staff is also in question. In 1996, the provincial government requests that interested teachers apply for early retirement/compensation packages. Although many teachers at Fernwood apply for these packages, at the end of the year the provincial government announces that no money exists, at least at the moment, to award the packages and thus decisions are deferred at least until 1997. Simultaneously, many teachers and administrators are actively pursuing positions at other schools and in many cases considering emigrating, primarily to Australia or New Zealand. Fernwood, with its stressful, conflict-ridden atmosphere, was becoming in Terry Pieters' words "the graveyard of every good teacher." Many of the teachers and administrators wish they were elsewhere; a significant proportion also began to actively imagine and plan for a life outside of Fernwood, and often outside of South Africa.

These major uncertainties and instabilities, compounded by the daily reality of living in a country in transition, create a situation in which nothing feels solid. On several occasions the headmaster would announce a new provincial or school policy one day only to announce a reversal or shift the next. Overall there is a strong sense that in a time of provincial and national change, consolidation, and chaos, Fernwood and other schools are left on their own to muddle through. In 1996, there is only minimal state imposition on Fernwood's daily operations, yet staff meetings are often full of warnings of what will happen the following school year when many of the new policies take effect. Some of these policies will force Fernwood to racially integrate its staff. Other policy changes, such as in the composition of the governing board of the school to make it more democratic and representative, will also be required, prompting further speculation, concern, and some fear. Because many of the administrators, and a fair number of teachers, had plans (or at least fantasies) of not working at Fernwood the following year, there was little active planning for or engagement with these changes. 1996 became, for many administrators and teachers at Fernwood, the year that marked the end of an era in terms of the school (as a Model C school) having control over the majority of its affairs. The state's imposition on Fernwood would only start in earnest in 1997, and thus many saw 1996 as their last opportunity for escape.

While all other schools in KwaZulu-Natal and in general throughout the country had to cope with the same level of external indecision and lack of guidance, Fernwood's chaotic and splintered community becomes a zone of collision. These collisions are multiple: Management collides with itself and with teachers; teachers fragment into multiple coalitions and align unevenly with and against management; students collide with each other and with teachers and management. Within these collisions over the daily practices of the school are embodied larger conflicts about continuity and change: the shift from an authoritarian past to a democratic future; the definition of teacher and student; the governance of the school; the coordinates of its identity. Most centrally for this book, the meaning of race is destabilized and contested in an environment saturated and struggling with how to recognize and engage difference.

CHAPTER FOUR

SHIFTING GROUND:

THE CHANGING CONTEXT OF RACE AT FERNWOOD

Within the conflict-ridden, tense, and uncertain atmosphere of Fernwood in 1996, the discursive construction of race plays a key role in school dynamics. Race does not exist solely as a preformed object, but is specifically shaped and molded within the particular context of Fernwood. The first half of this chapter examines how administrators and teachers produce race—how they attempt to orchestrate the production of both "black" and "white." [1] "Black" (here, African) and "white" are constructed as spaces of identity that are not simply old reworkings of apartheid categorizations, but new constructions that respond to the specificity of a moment of transition, both at Fernwood and in South Africa. The second half focuses on the shifting ground that constitutes the lives of Fernwood students. Students do respond to and, in some instances, resist the discursive construction of race perpetrated by the teachers and administrators. But, more crucially, new circumstances collide with the remnants of old—producing a terrain that differs markedly from that of the teachers. Here, I lay the groundwork for the remainder of the book, which is concerned with how youth maintain, recreate, and reshape the meaning of race.

PRODUCING WHITE

Though the majority of Fernwood's population in 1996 is black, the management persists in actively producing a "white" identity for the school. Here, I emphasize that whiteness is not simply a natural state, but a particular position that is, as Michelle Fine (1997) argues, "manufactured, in part, through institutional arrangements" (p. 58; see also Chalmers, 1997; Dyer, 1997; Fine, Weis, Powell, & Wong, 1997; Frankenberg, 1997; Hill, 1997; Proweller, 1998). [2] This whiteness is detached from any relation to the nation-state of South Africa. Instead, it is linked to two imagined spaces and refuges of whiteness: a local whiteness that resides in the practices of elite Durban schools, and a global whiteness that resides in the remnants of British Empire. By attempting to create a white identity articulated both above and below the nation-state, the school (as an institution) actively rejects an engagement with the emerging discourse of the rainbow nation or the practices of a newly democratic state.

Seeking White Bodies

Fernwood must construct its whiteness in several ways, the most basic of which is to recruit white bodies. Without white students, Fernwood would become, as many teachers comment, an "inner-city black school." White students, despite their academic and in some cases disciplinary history, become precious commodities as they provide the necessary reason for and link to the world of whiteness. In this case Fernwood, as a school, must accept the coevalness of its white students at least in public, though in private these same students are often both pitied and rejected because of their class status and generally poor academic achievement.

Despite this private reality, these white bodies become the only possible connection between Fernwood and the whiteness that the management desires. In the past Fernwood had maintained these links, though tenuously at times, with the more prestigious white schools in Durban through a shared legal designation and administrative structure. As Fernwood's black population grows larger, its already shaky connections to this larger world of whiteness, a perceived haven and refuge from the encroaching blackness, becomes weaker. Through the recruitment and retention of white bodies, Fernwood is not trying to simply hold on to its status from an earlier era. Fernwood was never part of the mainstream, elite white schools of Durban. Thus, the current management's concern is not to maintain the school's position within a certain field, but to build and create a position where none existed before.

But why are white bodies necessary for the production of whiteness? After all, the history of colonialist education practices is evidence that black or brown bodies can be schooled to identify with ruling white elites (Altbach & Kelly, 1984; Mangan, 1993). In fact, many of the more prestigious white schools in Durban continue to operate on this model, admitting only the children of the black upper and middle classes, who can be counted on to replicate, not challenge, predominant values.

But this model cannot work for Fernwood for several reasons. First, Fernwood's growing black population is predominantly working-class and poor. They come to school
with values and ways of life honed not in the elite suburbs but in the (poorer sections of) townships. Second, when these black students arrive at Fernwood, there is
not, as there is at other white schools, a cohort of white students whose behavior
can be replicated and followed (at least in management's imagination). Instead black
students meet white students who are poor, disruptive, and disengaged from the academic process. Fernwood lacks a core of white students who would create and
"model" the correct deportment, behavior, and so on for black students. In any case,
the black students, in numbers alone, are clearly in a position to lead, not follow,
when it comes to establishing parameters for behavior and action.

But Fernwood does not only recruit white bodies. In addition, it also constructs spaces of whiteness, safely detached from the nation-state of South Africa,
that attempt to consolidate the school's identity.

Constructing "Us": Sports as Identity

At the end of the fourth period, seconds before the bell rings for lunch break, there
is an announcement over the school intercom: All boys must report to a meeting
during the upcoming break. Annoyed, as my planned interview with a boy would
now have to be rescheduled, I decide to attend the meeting. As I walk down towards
the open area in the back of the school where the meeting was to be held I guess
that its purpose may be disciplinary and remember a mandatory meeting for girls
last week when they were reprimanded for the filthy state of the girls' toilets.

After the boys are lined up and quiet, Gene du Plessis, the head of the English department and a member of the school's administration, begins lecturing the
boys about the importance of rugby to the school:

> Rugby is the most visible sport at Fernwood. We get a couple hundred people
> to come to the games on Saturday morning; there's no sport that has that pro-
> file. The rugby scores are in the newspaper; they are visible. It is important
> that Fernwood has a good rugby team to field.

This pep talk for rugby and its importance to the school is followed by the
announcement that there would be compulsory rugby tryouts for all boys later that
week, and that all boys, regardless of their other athletic or academic commit-
ments, would play rugby. This type of assembly is repeated sporadically throughout the first half of the year as boys refuse to show up for the rugby tryouts and
practices and the administration becomes increasingly angry and adamant that all
boys will play rugby and enjoy it. This call for boys' mandatory participation dominates the school's relationship with its male students: John Gore, the third deputy
vice-principal, often commandeers the regular school assemblies (Monday and
Friday) to lecture, and usually yell until his face turns bright red, about the necessity of boys' participation in rugby.

The emphasis on sports, and rugby in particular, has historical roots in the white communities in Natal, which, as former British colonists, trace their passion for rugby to England and the traditions of English private boys' schools (Randall, 1982). [3] As Robert Morrell (1996) argues, rugby at white boys' schools in Natal allows upper-class white males to solidify their race, class, and gender position. Through the practice of rugby they inscribe an identity that can be clearly marked as different from that of poorer whites, blacks, and women. While historically Fernwood's emphasis on rugby may have served to bolster (however feebly) Fernwood's lagging class position in Durban, in 1996, Fernwood's management is more desperate to consolidate its racial identity. Most critically, Fernwood desires to see itself as comparable to the prestigious boys' schools, both private and public, that dominate the rugby imagination of Natal. Without rugby, cricket, netball, and athletics, Fernwood would no longer be visible as a white school.
Like students, many teachers are unenthusiastic about compulsory sports. Warren Korte connects the issue of sports to Fernwood's need to create a new identity:

> I think it's to try and find a new identity. It's to shed its old tradition and to find a new one. And I think if it does find a new one it can become the model school for South Africa. But it has to do away with its old traditions: enforcing sport and enforcing cricket, and enforcing those white ideas of rugby and of girls having to do netball.

Many staff resent the time that they are expected to spend on sports as coaches and referees for sports they often know or care little about. Jeanne Deacon links rugby to both issues of race and gender:

> Our management is very stereotypically South African chauvinist. They say yes, yes, pay lip service to it [issues of cultural diversity] but it's not as important as playing the rugby fixture . . . . We are very much locked into the old stereotypes of wanting to be a Southwood and a North Boys' High and what have you, based on the Eton-type thing.

The white symbolic of rugby works above and below the level of the nation at Fernwood. Although only one year before, in 1995, South Africa's victory in the World Cup had served to publicly unify (at least in some spaces) the nation, rugby at Fernwood refuses these coordinates. It disarticulates the tenuous relationship between rugby and the newly democratic nation (Steenvald & Strelitz, 1998), instead articulating rugby to a race and gender-exclusive practice. Rugby becomes symbolically situated as a local practice of white Durban and Natal and a global practice that is rooted in Britain but spread throughout the British Commonwealth. In this framework rugby cannot serve to unify but only to divide the school from its students.

In promoting rugby the school also resists the institutionalization of other sports, such as soccer and basketball, which are popular with the majority black students. For example, despite the basketball team's impressive season record and its multiracial composition, it receives scant attention or emphasis at school assemblies—it does not take its rightful place as one of the coordinates for the school's identity and pride. The resistance to basketball is strong at a governing board meeting, as the members discuss the possibility of replacing the substandard basketball court with a new one. Board members express concerns about the costs involved in the new court; although the school has the money, many feel that basketball may prove to be a passing fad and a few years hence they will be saddled with the "white elephant" of a basketball court. While rugby and cricket may be, in reality, the "white elephants" of the sports program, money is still invested without question into those sports. The blackness of the school is thus contained through the board's refusal to invest in proper facilities.

Despite the students' blatant resistance to sports and rugby, coupled with substantial staff opposition, sports occupies a central discursive place in the school's identity. The debate over sports, perhaps more than any other issue at the school, defines Fernwood's crisis as its management tries to desperately salvage its identity as a white school, unwilling to face the needs and desires of its current students.

STANDARDS

Like rugby, the issue of standards at Fernwood works to promote and solidify the school's whiteness at both the local and global levels. Fernwood's management imagines the school as part of a strata of schools in Durban and more broadly in South Africa that together constitute an elite that has more in common with the elite of other British Commonwealth countries than with other South African schools. This split is often posed in terms of the "First World" versus the "Third World" and Fernwood is symbolically positioned as a protector of specific First World standards in a nation that is slipping into the Third. The discourse of standards, most frequently, refers to issues of behavior and dress. [4]

School rules require that students wear their blazers to school on Monday and Friday; on Tuesday to Thursday, students are allowed to wear either the blazer, a school track jacket (available for purchase), or, in the case of matriculants, a special matriculant jacket, which is a casual, baseball-style jacket. Early in June, distressed by the continual violation of these rules, the headmaster talks at length during the assembly about the importance of wearing blazers and the image of the school. Despite this warning, dozens of students, each Monday and Friday, do not wear their blazers to school and are punished by being made to sit on the stage during assembly and to stay in for the break and after school. This ongoing, tedious process continues twice a week as the students routinely disobey management's orders. Finally, the last day of the third term arrives, a Friday, and with it school assembly. Many students are not in school (at least 100 are absent), and of those who are there another 100 or so don't have their blazers. Fuming, deputy vice-principal John Gore takes the stage and orders everyone without a blazer to remain after assembly. The rest of the school is sent back to their home classrooms, where they await individual dismissal by grade level. I leave with a group of matric students and go back with them to their classroom. As we sit in the classroom, talking and making plans for the upcoming holiday, there is an announcement that all students must return to the hall. Mr. Gore is on stage, awaiting our arrival—he has become even more infuriated as many of the students ordered to stay after the assembly did not, and others were passed blazers through the hall windows. Ranting and yelling, the search for students without blazers continues until Mr. Gore is satisfied that most have been apprehended. Finally the rest of the school is dismissed.

While the above example is the most extreme, throughout the year the importance of appearance and the image of the school is a constant mantra: recited endlessly at assemblies despite the obvious resistance of the students. Like sports, the Fernwood uniform operates, for the management, as a symbolic connection to the whiteness of Durban. The uniform connects Fernwood to other white schools (who enforce uniform requirements with little or no difficulty), and separates Fernwood from African, coloured, and Indian schools, where uniform policies are unevenly enforced. During the weeks I spent at a coloured and then Indian, school, I noticed that students routinely added bright sweaters, colored socks, jewelry, and other items to the school uniform. Within Durban the symbolism is clear: White schools enforce tight dress codes, other schools do not. For Fernwood, clinging to a uniform becomes one of the few ways it can tie to a local whiteness.

But this emphasis on appearance also ties it to a global standard that emanates from the private school world of Britain and spreads throughout the (former) colonies. It is this world of whiteness, separated and disconnected from a black South Africa, to which Fernwood desperately clings.

PRODUCING BLACK

Although in previous years Fernwood's relatively poor white students would have been constructed as other, the management must now, at least publicly, embrace these same white students. Instead, African students, of all class positions, become confined by discursive practices that are virtually impossible to escape: They become the other. Here, I emphasize that ". . . the Other is never simply given, never just found or encountered, but *made*" (Fabian, 1990, p. 755, emphasis is the author's). Just as a specific whiteness is produced in an attempt to stave off the inevitable changes that will eventually transform the school, a "blackness" must similarly be manufactured. Again, the discursive construction of blackness both draws on and moves beyond apartheid constructions.

While the production of whiteness is largely a management project, teachers are significantly more implicated in the discourses that produce blackness. This is not to imply that the processes are separate; in fact, they work in tandem. But teachers, because of the frustrations they experience in the classroom every day (due in no small part to the management's "whiteness" project), are more willing and are well positioned to accept and perpetuate the circulating discourses of blackness.

The construction of blackness at Fernwood rests on the discourse of authenticity, which negates the other by strategically denying their coevalness. As Cameron McCarthy et al. (1997) argue, drawing on Friedrich Nietzsche, this practice of resentment is a "strategy of negating the other and the tactical and strategic deployment of moral evaluation and emotion" (p. 84). Culture is deployed as a trope to signify a difference that is fixed and immobilized. Difference is not simply marked, but, as McCarthy et al. point out, becomes a way in which moral judgements and evaluations are made. In this case, the production of blackness through a discourse of authenticity ensures that whiteness (despite the shifts in its constitution) remains a space of superiority.

IMAGINING ZULUNESS: THE CONSTRUCTION OF AUTHENTICITY

A Wednesday morning, and Mr. du Plessis' grade 11 English class is discussing Chinua Achebe's *Things Fall Apart*. Or perhaps it would be more accurate to say that Mr. du Plessis is talking and students are doing anything but listening—doodling, talking to neighbors, sleeping, and doing homework seem to be of more interest to these students than the book. But Mr. du Plessis forges on; he told me earlier, before class, that he is particularly excited about teaching *Things Fall Apart* to this class (composed solely of African students) as he feels that they will be able to identify with the book's themes and characters.

Mr. du Plessis' attempts to prod students to draw parallels between the Ibo traditions discussed in the book and the indigenous, Zulu traditions that he assumes are part of the daily lives of his students. Ethnically the vast majority of Africans in Durban would identify as Zulu and that reality is also reflected at Fernwood. But this morning Mr. du Plessis is having difficulty. Finally he asks the girls in the class if they regularly attended the reed dance, which he understands to be a traditional Zulu custom. Only one girl answers and says, "This is the 90s," which prompts generalized laughter in the class, vigorous agreement from other girls, and a renewed round of talking and note passing. Later on many of the students tell me that they think *Things Fall Apart* is "old-fashioned" and has no relevance to their lives despite Mr. du Plessis' insistence on parallels.

This "imagined Zuluness" is a key element of the discourse of authenticity that serves to produce blacks in the white imagination at Fernwood. This difference, which denies the coevalness of blacks and whites, positions the school and white culture as "dynamic and oriented towards change," while reinscribing Zulu culture as representative of non-Western cultures that "seek equilibrium and the reproduction of inherited forms" (Clifford, 1987, p. 125). This construction of African students pervades all aspects of the school's practices.

For example, the only space in which African students are allowed some measure of self-expression and responsibility is within the Zulu choir, which performs sporadically at school assemblies and special occasions. The members of the choir, who are extremely talented and disciplined, practice on their own as the teacher who supervised them previously no longer works at Fernwood. Teachers, for the most part, applaud their efforts and there are often suggestions that the choir deserves more support from the school as a whole. But the success of the choir and a group of African students who participate in Zulu dancing, describe in large part the white staff's understanding of the identity of its students.

Frozen in time, African students are rarely allowed to enter the 1990s, to exist within a constantly flowing cultural stream that shifts and changes, affected by the processes of modernization, globalization, economic inequality, and political realignment. The school and its students collide as staff relies on cultural difference to explain its difficulty reaching students. While staff try to fix students' selves in the ethnic practices of Zuluness, students' identities are defined through their situatedness within modernity. For example, Zondi speaks back to white constructions of African identities:

> People automatically assume that just because I am black, I have a real tradition. My family doesn't go around slaughtering cows or sheep on special occasions as many white people believe. I consider that a thing that my ancestors did in the past . . . . I enjoy traditional Zulu dancing and singing. To dance I have to practise though.

Zondi does not reject part of her cultural identity as Zulu but neither does she naturalize it—her facility with Zulu dancing, like any other skill, must be learned and perfected through practice. Debra, another African student, both laments and rejects aspects of what she sees as traditional Zulu culture:

> I see myself as a young teenager who sees the whole world going down the drain. No one follows their cultures anymore. We are so combined . . . . I know very little about my culture. As I see it today there is no one who keeps their culture anymore. In South Africa we are so combined. I live in a civilized way. I prefer it than the olden days ways of living. I wouldn't imagine myself walking half naked like they used to be, going to the bushes getting some wood and even getting married in a traditional way—no ways!

Debra regrets the loss of traditional culture, and at the same time makes it clear that she is comfortable with her contemporary lifestyle. In contrast to the Fernwood staff's perception of African identity, Debra embraces modernity and sees herself as constituted by it.

Finally, Neville, also an African student, expresses a similar tension between, as he defines it, the West and Africa:

> I see myself partially Westernized and still partially African. I don't consider myself as a person who knows a lot about my culture and my roots because of the modern world we are living in, but nobody is to blame because I accept change . . . . I take all my cultural and traditional customs seriously and will carry on practising them as my family still carries them out.

As these quotes suggest, African students at Fernwood do not position themselves either as guardians of or repositories for, "authentic" Zulu culture. The localized, cultural authenticity constructed by Fernwood staff represents only one, relatively small, coordinate of identity for African students. Many African students are puzzled by the white staff's attempts to mark them through their connection to their Zulu identity, as it is not, in most cases, the way in which they define themselves. Yet, for the Fernwood staff, "culture" often becomes a simple, comfortable marker for understanding the differences between white staff and African students. Race, as a complex historical, political, social, and economic phenomenon is avoided, and instead the trope of "culture" pervades Fernwood staff's engagement with its African students. The omnipresent explanation of "cultural difference" overwhelms discussions of black students, contributing to an environment in which all black children are constructed as Third World others, who embody an inferior internal logic that must be tamed within the First World environs of the school. Blackness is not an empty category, but one that is produced against whiteness through understanding African students as static cultural icons, instead of dynamic youth positioned both materially and discursively within modernity (see Soudien, 1998).

THE CONTEXT OF CHANGE:
FERNWOOD STUDENTS MEET THE NEW SOUTH AFRICA

Fernwood students are the vanguard. Although the majority of South African youth still live and study in racially segregated environments, Fernwood students experience the raw novelty of desegregation every day. They are encircled by national discursive appeals to ethnic and racial respect and tolerance (the rainbow nation), and to the fresh opportunities that surround them (the new South Africa). But most are unimpressed, skeptical that much has changed in South Africa, and pessimistic that substantial transformation is possible. Melissa, a coloured student, comments, "I'm not sure about South Africa being a rainbow nation; to me it's just like, it hasn't changed. It's just the same to me: the whites be with the whites, the blacks be with the blacks." Melissa's observation about the pervasive racial separation at Fernwood is borne out during every break period, as students divide by race on the playing field. Exceptions to this pattern are rare. Jill, a white student, is aware of South Africa's international reputation for racial harmony, but disagrees: "People come to South Africa, they see all the cultures, they see all the races, but not all of them get along . . . . There's always that racial barrier between, some people will always keep that racial barrier. It's like grudges." Dumisani, an African student, defines the problem as racism, not racial barriers:

> To be a rainbow nation, everything has to get right. And you find you have racism, an element of racism. So I think it's far from being a rainbow nation . . . . I think it's going to take a decade to get where it should be. People might say it's a rainbow nation, but I really don't think so.

Many students believe that a rainbow nation is an unobtainable goal. Nikki, a coloured student, remarks:

> They want to make everybody one big happy family, and it's not going to work. People have different ideas. I know it takes all kinds to make the world, and how we are going to work in harmony. But that's a whole lot of hogwash, when it boils down to the fact that you cannot, no matter how hard you try, it's not going to work. Making a rainbow nation and that sort of thing.

Samantha, a white girl, agrees, "No matter how hard we try, we can never, as they say, form one, because those differences will always come between us. And it's sad, because it's a lovely thought, all working together, but it will never happen."

Students' pessimism flows from many sources—one of the most significant is the constant threat of violence, which dominates and restricts everyday life. For most students at Fernwood, of all races, violence is a constant presence that they can neither explain nor imagine life without. Systemic, state-sponsored violence has long been a part of South Africa: the violence of forced removals, of deaths in state detention, of children murdered at Soweto, of apartheid itself. For Fernwood students, that form of violence is history: events that they are only vaguely aware of, if at all, and that seemingly have no connection to the present. The violence of their lives is personal and intimate: gun battles in the streets outside their houses, a friend raped, a neighbor carjacked and murdered.

Durban and the entire province has attracted national and often worldwide attention because of ongoing political violence, instigated by the Inkatha Freedom Party (IFP), and supported, in large measure, by the former white government (Farred, 1992). During the long years of the 1980s and early 1990s, the Nationalist government armed and trained the IFP as part of its plan to destabilize and delegitimize the African National Congress (ANC). In KwaZulu-Natal, nearly 13,000 people, particularly in the rural areas and African townships, were murdered in the ensuing violence that continued through the time of this research. The violence also caused massive displacement as people fled villages and townships that were no longer safe: It is estimated that over 500,000 people were displaced in 1994 (Louw & Sekhonyane, 1997).

In the townships that are home to many Fernwood students, there still exist "no go" areas that are off-limits to supporters of either the IFP or ANC. In addition to this politically motivated violence, there are the crimes, gangs, and shootings associated with downward spirals of poverty and despair. Although no Fernwood student I questioned was able to explain the causes of the ongoing violence, it was accepted as a constant feature of their lives. Michelle reflects, "I've never known of people not fighting, like violence like they have in Soweto and all that .... It's not new, but it's not old either. It's just something that's always been there." Molefe, who lives in the township of Umlazi, explains:

> It will take a long time for me to get over what I have experienced in the past .... if you live in the township you experience murder each and every day.

> Even in my township if you see a person carrying a gun you don't get worried
> because you've seen that thing so many times, and so many people are killed
> it doesn't bother you a little bit.

Not understanding the historical, economic, and political circumstances
that cause and perpetuate the violence, some students are quick to blame the new
government. From their perspective, the end of apartheid has coincided with a
rise in violence. While absolute numbers may not have risen and in some cases
have dropped, perceptions have changed dramatically, as the violence that was
once confined to the townships now seeps well beyond those borders. Many violent crimes actually declined in the period 1994–1996. For example, murder
declined from 66.6 per 100,000 of the population in 1994, to 61.1 per 100,000 in
1996. Robbery with aggravated circumstances dropped from 210.8 to 159.2 per
100,000. But other crimes have increased. Incidents of rape were up from 105.3
per 100,000 in 1994, to 119.5 in 1996. Residential housebreaking also increased
from 566 per 100,000 in 1994 to 583.6 per 100,000 in 1996 (Crime Information
Management Centre, 1997; see also *The Mercury*, 1996). Furthermore, the police
themselves were found to be at the center of many of the violent crimes in South
Africa in the 1990s, including coordinating notorious car hijacking rings in the
Johannesburg area (A. Johnson, 1996). Many whites may be benefiting tremen-
dously from what is often perceived as a "black crime wave."

Despite this mixed reality, white, coloured, and Indian students are often con-
vinced that the heightened danger they feel is a reflection of growing African crim-
inal behavior. Violent behavior, crime, and murder become associated with Africans,
particularly African men. White, coloured, and Indian girls admit to crossing the
street if they are approaching an African man, and frequently complain about being
harassed by African, and sometimes coloured, men when they are in town. Violence
perpetuated by Africans, both physical and sexual, becomes a critical component of
the way in which white students, and to a large, though sometimes more conflicted
extent, coloureds and Indians, interpret their lives in the new South Africa.

Hazel, an Indian student, believes that her life would have been safer and
more stable during apartheid. When I ask her what would have been different for
her if she had been a high school student in 1986, instead of 1996, she replies:

> With apartheid we all had our places. I mean Indians wouldn't steal from each
> other, whites wouldn't steal from each other, blacks wouldn't steal from each
> other. It would have been safe in 1986, it was safe in 1986, but now it's not
> safe to go anywhere, it's not safe to do anything, you know. Your life isn't
> assured anymore.

Purity, an African student, directly blames the new government for the rise in
violent crime:

> The rate of crime [is out of hand] because you know the people who disobey
> the law get favored by the courts, they go to jail for a short period. . . . . [Under

the old government] the rate of crime was better, because they could get the criminals, the violence and stuff. People were sent to jail and they got the punishment they deserved.

For blacks with the financial resources, one response to rising crime is to escape the township for the formerly white areas, which are still perceived as relatively safe. Although parents may appreciate the quiet and refuge of the white areas, the students miss their friends and crave the excitement of the townships. Numbuso comments:

> In the white suburbs, it's quiet; nothing goes on there. It's dead. . . . . Mostly in the black townships there are guns. You live with them, you're not far away from them. Police running after people, it's a bit, it's chaotic. And I like chaos.

Numbuso and other students have an ambivalent relationship towards violence, both recognizing and guarding against its danger, but simultaneously embracing it. Muriel, a coloured student who recently moved to a white suburb, expresses a similar sentiment:

> There's no people in Seaview [the suburb where she now lives], everybody's like locked inside their houses like they fear to come outside, like somebody's going to eat them or something. It's true, that's what they do. You ask anyone.

Muriel rightly perceives the growing fear in the community surrounding Fernwood. In June, a woman who lives in a house near the school is murdered in her kitchen during a burglary. Several months later, a man is carjacked in his driveway: the car is stolen and he is murdered. Both attacks take place during daylight.

Nor is Fernwood immune from violence and death. During the year I spent there, three members of the Fernwood community (two students and a library aide, a recent Fernwood graduate) are killed: two in car accidents, one allegedly during a drug deal. Even the walk from the bus stop to school is sometimes not safe: late in the year, a girl from the matric class, Melody, is attacked as she walks alone through the park next the school. The park has become a haven for the homeless and students are warned not to walk alone, but on this morning Melody's friends are late and she decides to walk by herself. Melody manages to escape the man who attacks her, and arrives at school shaken and dirty, with torn clothing.

Violence also impacts dramatically on students' social lives. Clubs are particularly dangerous, as evenings out are sometimes interrupted by gun battles. Very few African students at Fernwood will venture into most of the predominantly African clubs in town; they know that it can potentially be very dangerous. Sipho comments that "you only go to those clubs if you want to say good-bye to the planet." Girls in particular speak frequently about the risk of being raped in these clubs or any time they go into town at night. Dressing cautiously, as Octavia elaborates, is necessary:

You can't wear a skirt, like a short skirt, because rape is very likely . . . . It's
safer to go out with trousers on, you feel more comfortable about what you are
wearing. It's easier to run, and you don't attract attention to yourself . . . . You
know the dangers of bringing attention to yourself at night.

The coloured clubs are also notorious for their gang-related violence, and
some coloured students frequent the white clubs for this reason. As Charles
explains, going to the coloured clubs involves some risk:

We go to the coloured clubs as well; we like them. But it's a bit dangerous,
there are always shooting and stabbings and stuff. Two of my friends were actually killed in coloured discos. But people go.

Charles and other coloured students treat this particular facet of violence
as unique to coloureds (though it is not) and as an important attribute of their
identity. For example, many of the younger coloured girls at Fernwood have formed
gangs; one of the more prominent ones is the VDGs (Vatican Destruction Girls),
so named because they hate silence and aim to destroy it.

Given the violence, and the political and economic instability of South Africa
in 1996, few Fernwood students are optimistic about their futures. For some students,
particularly whites, the perception of an ever-increasing crime rate is a reason to
think about leaving South Africa. Samantha expresses her fears about the future:

That's another reason I'm thinking of leaving, is the violence . . . . People getting stabbed. I heard about this robbery, this guy got held up at an ATM, they
took his money and they actually came back to shoot him. I don't understand
how people can steal, how people can kill.

Many white students see little future in South Africa for themselves or the children
they may have one day and, like the white teachers and administrators at Fernwood,
disconnect themselves from identification with the nation. Peter, a matric student,
expressed his, and many of his classmates', desire to leave South Africa:

You look at Durban, and you look at something like Mauritius or England,
this is like a fourth world country compared to England and I'd rather move
up there. Even America's better than this . . . . We've got cars they thought
of like eight years ago, their movies come out first, I just think it's better in
America and England.

The instability and change that these students have experienced in their lives and
uncertainty about the future lead some students to fear continual chaos. Jackie,
another white student, comments:

Everything seems to fall apart. The government, there's such a problem with
government at this moment, because I feel like whichever government is put
into power, there will be a revolution, there will be upheaval, about half the
population will not be happy with it, so we are going to have serious problems.

White students, similar to the white teachers and administrators, are in general scared of the future and skeptical that they will be able to have what they consider normal lives in South Africa. Jackie views this situation in global terms, feeling that the violence she sees around her will only escalate. As a rap music fan, she easily draws parallels between South Central Los Angeles and South Africa:

> It's like thinking about what could probably happen to South Africa in a couple of years, we will probably have gangs like that doing stuff, because it seems almost inevitable that is what is going to come to South Africa.

Gary, another white student, also clings to South Africa in the belief that there is no place that is better:

> A lot of people say there's no future, and this country's got nothing. But I believe that if you give this country time it'll change . . . . I feel that in any country anywhere in the world you'll find mostly the same problems . . . . I think people just have fear of what's going to happen, and they want to run. But then people will find it's just as bad wherever they go.

African students, more than white, coloured, or Indian students, are somewhat hopeful about their futures in South Africa. But most are not euphoric about staying there, instead emphasizing the need for hard work, both individually and collectively as a nation. Thobile comments:

> We are trying to work together, but it is a difficult thing because we are just starting the new South Africa so it's not easy for these young people, like whites, to just like to take it, because it's new for us.

Purity is not particularly committed to South Africa, but feels that at least she now has a chance at a decent life, "I'm not quite happy with it [staying here], but if I just work hard academically I think I'll find a good job and be able to, you know, get stable with my life." Many African students would consider job opportunities in other countries if the situation arose—the elimination of apartheid has opened up not just South Africa, but the whole world. Molefe, who is from a politically active family, feels more strongly about South Africa than most African students. But he too admits that his passion for his nation is not necessarily the predominant one in the African community:

> Some black people want to leave because they say we've suffered too much and now we want to live in luxury. Because they see on tv, correct me if I'm wrong, but when you see a house in the U.S. you always see a double story house, a white picket fence, three cars, and three kids, two boys and a girl. And the father is the head of this huge company, and the mother is the head of this huge company. And people just see the tv and they think the U.S. is that.

Amidst general feelings of pessimism and indifference, there are exceptions. Amanda, the head girl, [5] who is of Indian and coloured background, realizes that her hope is a minority opinion:

I'm proud that I'm a South African, and like in the prefects' room, a lot of the prefects say they want to get out of this country, this country has no future. The way I'm looking at it I'm South African and it's what I make of it . . . . So I can join the rat race and just leave, or I can stay here, and make something for myself.

Unwilling participants in the process of change in South Africa, Fernwood students are unenthusiastic about their nation's future, and skeptical about the promise of racial harmony. For white students, the administration's "whiteness" project does little to address their everyday concerns about life in a multiracial democracy; for black students, this same project minimizes the complexity of their lives and provides them with few opportunities.

WORLDS APART

Although they exist side-by-side, in daily, constant contact, the lives of Fernwood staff and students are profoundly, radically, separate. The Fernwood administration tries to perpetuate and reinvent the only world they know, one in which excellence in rugby and immaculate school uniforms are paramount. Whiteness is their world, and they are determined to ensure that Fernwood is "white." Fernwood's whiteness, unquestioned just six years earlier, is now at risk, and its local and global markers must not be simply maintained, but given new life. The climate they create at Fernwood both mocks and challenges the racial harmony promoted by the government, as the administration (and many, though not all, teachers) are uninterested in moving forward into the new.

Students, in contrast, have little choice. Their lives are not, and cannot, be defined by the retreat to whiteness. Both black and white are thrown into a world in upheaval: one in which the racial divides of apartheid are both absent and fiercely present, where violence pervades everyday life, where futures are insecure. Race is still a vital category of organization and identity for students, and its existence produces clashes, not peaceful coexistence. Yet simultaneously race does not exist in the same form as it once did. In the following chapter, I will turn my attention to the complexities of this transformation of race.

CHAPTER FIVE

CREATING RACE:

THE ROLE OF TASTE IN YOUTH'S PRODUCTION OF IDENTITIES

Bolstered by a conflict-ridden school and society, race persists as a crucial aspect of students' lives. Nonracial harmony and the cheery hand-holding of the "rainbow nation" give way to the stark reality of continued divisions and inequality. But for Fernwood students, race is also rearticulated within the context of a new historical moment. Race, and racial identity, is no longer tied to apartheid-driven cultural absolutes, but instead rotates around the axes of political and social change in South Africa, and the globalizing forces of late modernity and postmodernity. Increasingly, race is constituted and driven by a discourse of taste, which locates identity within the commodity culture nurtured through global popular culture.

PLACE AND IDENTITY

Among Fernwood students, there is a sense of significant shifts in the constitution of selves. For example, African students are poised at a three-way juncture: an ever-changing traditional culture that exists for many only in the imagination; the urbanization of modernity; and the globalizing thrust of postmodernity. [1] Identity is patched together from sources that bubble up all over the globe; new spaces open as youth and youth cultures become what Doreen Massey (1998) refers to as a "product of interaction." African students at Fernwood call on the icons and symbols of the global popular to rework racial identities. Lerato, for example, confounds the notion of an African identity rooted in the isolated dynamics of the local, as she writes:

> I have a style and a total niche in fashion. I revolve around it. I love clothes which are designed by French designers, but that does not mean I don't support our African fashion. As a person, I don't believe I should have African clothing just because I live in Africa, that is totally not my individual identity.

Here, Lerato conflates taste (or what she terms style) with identity, and insists that her identity will not be driven by the randomness of geographic location. While Lerato accesses the global popular to proclaim what she terms an "individual" identity, Vusi specifically discusses how race, and racialized identities, are constructed in this space:

> Our race is unique; we are multitalented because we can participate in all sports. There are many superstars who are of a black race, for example, Michael Jackson, Michael Jordan, etc. These are the people who are dedicated to their particular activities and most of all they are black. We are different the way we speak. We always seem to use slang no matter what language it is, for example, in South Africa we use tsotsi [gangster] language and in America they use slang.

For Vusi, the icons of the global popular, here Michael Jackson and Michael Jordan, are used to develop his sense of a racialized self. Many of the cultural forms that Vusi identifies with his race do not originate on the continent of Africa in a narrow, territorial sense, but instead in the cultural practices of African-Americans (see Gilroy, 1993, for a discussion of black global cultural flows).

Themba similarly unhinges African identity from South African (or African) soil, locating it in the practices of the global popular. He writes:

> Because we are a unique race, I feel proud. Here I am stressing out my pride about my race not only in South Africa, but internationally. We all seem to be acting and behaving the same and that shows we all have something in common. We play the same music with rhythm and the majority will wear the same fashions and that you can easily notice. We also prefer the same sports, e.g., soccer and basketball.

Although Themba may overstate the similarities among Africans (both in Africa and the diaspora), it is apparent that his sense of what it means to be African is multifaceted, and derived as much from global cultural symbols and form as from the material conditions of his life.

Emerging from these students' reflections is a sense of self that draws on the commodities, icons, and practices of global popular culture. Affective investments drive the manner in which the notion of African, in this case, is imagined. As I will discuss throughout this chapter, white, coloured, and Indian students also access the global popular in a similar manner.

The influence of the global popular simultaneously complicates how white students, for example, construct Africans. Discourses of cultural authenticity rooted in the local still exist, yet they do not exert the same explanatory power, and most critically must interact with new national and global realities that challenge these conceptions. The enormous influence of African-American popular culture, and figures such as Michael Jordan, Oprah Winfrey, and Tupac Shakur, complicate white students' positioning of their African classmates. In this milieu, it is more difficult for white students to deny the coevalness of their black classmates. Stereotypes of "primitiveness" must confront the modernity embedded in the African-American musicians, sports figures, and talk show hosts who populate the global stage and, in the minds of white students, exercise considerable global power. White students must also face new dynamics of power in their relationships with black students. No longer are whites necessarily wealthier than their black classmates, nor in the numerical majority at the school. Black students similarly confront a changing constellation of whiteness, as white Fernwood students disengage themselves from a nationally bounded white identity that looks to the markers of apartheid and instead reach outside of South Africa to access their "white" identity (see, e.g., my discussion of the school fashion show that follows later in this chapter).

These rapid changes in both the local and global terrain of race produce new twists in its construction. The global commodity, explained and policed through a discourse of taste, becomes the fulcrum for constructing one's own racialized identity, connecting self to others who are of a similar "race" and disconnecting from those who are of a different "racial" background. Culture, a paradigm ultimately tied to geography and a (relatively) centered and stable sense of place, can no longer fully "explain" racial difference. While culture is place-bound, taste's structures are not. Using taste enables an analysis of race that places it in global circulation, and within, not outside of, the global flows of popular culture and associated commodities.

THE DISCOURSE OF TASTE

The use of global commodities and popular icons to define self may not necessarily be a new phenomenon. [2] As I discussed in chapter 1, black South Africans have often looked outside of the borders of South Africa and the physical and mental bonds of apartheid to construct selves. While it is clear that taste may have been an important facet of identity, social structure, and scaffoldings of power in previous decades (i.e., the role it played in Sophiatown in the 1950s), it emerges within Fernwood in 1996 as the most critical public marking of collective racial identities. [3]

Working in a different context, Dick Hebdige (1979) charts British youth's resistance to dominant ideologies through an analysis of their style, defining youth subcultures as authentic spaces that resist the commoditized consumerism of mass culture. Clothes and accessories play a crucial role in Hebdige's analysis, as they serve as the basis for youth's constitution of oppositional selves. Theorizing in a feminist framework that emphasizes individual, not collective, identities, Judith Williamson (1986) comments on the importance of commodities to the definition of self (or selves):

> When I rummage through my wardrobe in the morning I am not merely faced
> with a choice of what to wear. I am faced with a choice of images . . . . You
> know perfectly well that you will be seen differently for the whole day, depending
> on what you put on; you will appear as a particular kind of woman with
> one particular identity, *which excludes others*.(p. 91, emphasis is the author's)

Thus, while it is well established that commodities are used as significant aspects of social, cultural, and political lives and identities, this research extends previous work. In contrast to the research of Hebdige and others associated with subculture research (see, e.g., Gelder & Thornton, 1997), my concern here is with commodities as expressions of selves, not as locations of resistance to parent cultures, dominant cultures, or mass culture. Unlike subcultures such as the teddy boys of the 1950s or the punks of the 1970s, Fernwood students do not mock and resist mass culture through reappropriating stylistic conventions.

Instead, these students employ commodities in multiple and at times contradictory ways—they both rearticulate predefined racial identities, and (deliberately and not) push at the borders of possible racial selves. Through their actions, or their "symbolic creativity" (Willis, 1990) they embrace commodities, consumer culture, capitalism, the pursuit of pleasure and the importance of affect.

This production of selves is located within what Pierre Bourdieu (1990) refers to as a habitus, which he describes as

> systems of durable, transposable dispositions, structured structures predisposed
> to function as structuring structures, that is, as principles which generate and
> organize practices and representations that can be objectively adapted to their
> outcomes without presupposin g a conscious aiming at ends or an express mastery
> of the operations necessary in order to attain them. (p. 53)

Bourdieu's notion of habitus allows for a freedom within particular parameters; it assures that structures will perpetuate, but never exactly replicate. Unlike rules, habitus does not presume conscious mastery of behavior, but allows for the adaptation of practices that in the end are productive of a new, yet enduring, habitus.

In Bourdieu's scholarship (1984), taste is a fundamental component of a habitus. Taste does not stand outside of social, economic, and political structures, nor is it a neutral matter of individual desire. Instead, taste functions as a "mediated preference," which reflects and produces (in Bourdieu's scholarship) the class distinctions and economic structures of a society. Although taste appears to be a matter of an individual's free choice, that "choice" is actually situated within complex structures that predetermine it. As Bourdieu uses the term, a particular taste in music and art, for example, "is an expression of an individual's objective location in systems of social classification and difference" (p. 417). Taste in Bourdieu's analysis is not peripheral or secondary to this process of class reproduction—it is constitutive of this process.

Bourdieu's scholarship, and his theorization of the relationship between taste and habitus, has been criticized for being overly deterministic (see, e.g., Fenster, 1991). What Bourdieu's large-scale, quantitative project fails to capture is the dynamism of taste and the way in which *taste itself* becomes the ground of struggle. Taste for Bourdieu remains a relatively static and enduring expression of social and economic location (within the temporal and spatial parameters of his study); he does not probe if and how taste changes, and the effects that these changes have on social structures.

But within my decidedly smaller project, and the confines of Fernwood, I am able to chart two trajectories of taste. First, taste operates to discursively recode race, and serves as the basis of race's rearticulation within Fernwood youth's globalized sense of self. But taste is simultaneously flimsy and unstable. As students negotiate a multiracial environment, they find that taste's borders move and shift on occasion. In these instances, taste ceases to be reproductive; instead taste points to and illuminates the breaks and changes in the racial construction of selves at Fernwood. Youth use taste in conflicting ways: to reproduce their positions within racialized structures, and simultaneously to challenge those positions, cracking open spaces for the emergence of new identities, locations, and forms.

These divergent forces in the use of taste at Fernwood are the focus of this chapter and the two that follow. In the remainder of this chapter, I map the fundamental ground of the racial politics of taste at Fernwood; in chapter 6, I turn to a discussion of the multiple ways that taste operates at Fernwood; and finally in chapter 7 I examine how taste plays a role in the ways in which individual students construct racialized identities.

CONSTRUCTING RACIALIZED SELVES

For Fernwood students, two aspects of popular culture are particularly vital to defining racialized selves: fashion and music. In a society and social structure that places emphasis on the construction of identities through commodities, clothing necessarily becomes more than a functional, utilitarian item. Instead, clothing is transformed through taste categories into a discourse of fashion, which in turn bears on the construction of racialized selves at Fernwood. As Jennifer Craik (1994) writes, "We can regard the ways in which we clothe the body as an active process or technical means for constructing and presenting a bodily self" (p.1). At Fernwood, collective racial selves are actively constructed by students through the selection, arrangement, and presentation of clothing. Music also plays a substantial role in the racial politics of Fernwood. But music, more than fashion, tends to erupt as a racial battleground within specific circumstances—for example, as I discuss in this chapter, during the school fashion show and school-sponsored discos.

As I begin this discussion of the role of fashion and music in the reproduction of race at Fernwood, it is important to emphasize that on a daily basis much of this production occurs only in the realm of the imagination (Appadurai, 1996). Fernwood students, like students at virtually every other school in South Africa, wear uniforms to school. Occasionally a "civvies" day is allowed, usually on the last day of the term or a holiday such as Valentine's Day, but in 1996 civvies days were deemed too disruptive to the functioning of the school and were eliminated. Yet clothing is so vital that students can often recall in vivid detail what they and others wore to school on these rare days, even several years ago. Music, quite obviously, also does not figure into the daily routine of school—Walkmans, radios, and boom boxes are strictly forbidden. Instead, the contours of its racial imaginary come into play outside of school and during specific school-sponsored events.

Though uniforms are required at school, students see each other in street clothes in town on weekends and holidays and occasionally at school social events. Town, with its clubs and discos, is also the arena for the meeting of different, racialized tastes in music. The social geography of "town" is a critical space for the generation of taste cultures and racialized identities. Although students are, in large measure, racially separated where they live, the downtown area of Durban is a space that is accessible to all. Buses and taxi [4] ranks located downtown provide access to all areas of the city and surrounding townships, and many students have to take one bus or taxi into the city from Fernwood (about a thirty-minute ride by bus) and then pick up a second bus or taxi to get home. Consequently, the downtown area, particularly the mall (the Workshop) located directly across from the bus stops and taxi ranks, is swarming with students in the late afternoon and all day on Saturday. However, very few Fernwood students actually live in town. Once an exclusively white area, the downtown area is now populated almost solely by blacks, as whites fled to the surrounding suburbs. Urban decay, coupled with rising crime levels, has also kept middle-class adults, of all races, wary of going into town at night. For many adolescents, on the other hand, "town" is the only lively, public space available on public transportation, and thus becomes a mecca, drawing teenagers from all over Durban. Many of the clubs frequented by students are in town, and the popular Saturday matinees at the coloured and Indian clubs (catering to the under-eighteen set) are packed. The streets surrounding the clubs, the Workshop, and the few movie theaters in town are jammed with coloured, Indian, and occasionally African students on a typical Saturday afternoon. African clubs in town are often considered dangerous, and African students at Fernwood are more likely than their white, Indian, and coloured classmates to stay closer to home on the weekend. African girls, however, will frequently go into town to shop on Saturday, the busiest shopping day of the week in Durban. White students are not seen as frequently in the club and Workshop area after school and on Saturdays, preferring to spend their time at the beach, a short walk from the center of town. Along the boardwalk, which is crammed with hotels, an amusement park, a swimming pool, dozens of restaurants and bars, and vendors of all kinds catering to tourists, white adolescents hang out on the sand tanning, and in the water, swimming and surfing. Surfing, and surf culture, is popular among many white teenagers, and their almost exclusive lock on the sport reflects both their economic privilege and the remnants of an apartheid system that reserved surfing beaches for whites only. More white adolescents flock to the city in the evening, as the techno and rave clubs open, and stay open often till 4 A.M.. After-hours clubs, which open at 1 or 2 A.M. and stay open all night, are also popular with white teenagers.

Despite the fact that students of all races share in using the space, resources, and entertainment offered by the center city, interaction among groups is fleeting. As many students explain, often they will meet up with Fernwood students of other races in town and stop to chat briefly or wave hello. But differing interests and priorities ultimately pull them in separate directions, away from sustained communication or interaction. Michelle, a coloured student, elaborates:

> You go into town, you'll only see coloureds with coloureds, whites with whites, Indians with Indians. But then like, but then if you meet up with the people from school we'll talk to them, but then we'll say we want to go here, and then they'll say no they don't want to go there, they want to go elsewhere . . . . Everybody's different.

Although these interracial meetings are brief and insubstantial, they are nonetheless important interactions, because it is here that students generate the taste differences that feed into the racialized selves that become fully formed and oppositional at Fernwood.

MAPPING FASHION

The borders that demarcate the different racialized groups at Fernwood are clearly defined through the practices of fashion. As Simon Frith (1996) argues in reference to music:

> What I want to suggest, in other words, is not that social groups agree on values which are then expressed in their cultural activities . . . . but that they only get to know themselves *as groups* . . . . *through* cultural activity, through aesthetic judgement, (p. 111, emphasis is the author's)

In other words, racialized groups at Fernwood do not choose particular fashions that reflect or represent their group, but the commodity, once it becomes associated with a particular group, is used to create and reinforce group solidarity. Amanda, a coloured girl, [5] comments, "You know if you meet a coloured boy because he wears a certain type of pants, a certain type of shoes, he dresses in a certain way, he acts a certain way." Coloured students, like whites, Africans, and Indians become defined through a pattern of "goods in their assemblage" (Douglas & Isherwood, 1979). [6] The goods, or more accurately the commodities, are extremely specific:

Only a relatively tiny universe of brands and taste preferences can be called on to invoke a racialized identity.

Coloured students, more than any other group at Fernwood, claim that their clothing style is significantly influenced by African-American fashion. Although many coloured students still harbor mixed feelings about Africans in South Africa, they demonstrate no such ambivalence about African-Americans, embracing and imitating their style. As Charles writes, "Teenage coloured boys have the most unique way of dressing. We tend to wear clothing which is closely related to the U.S.A.." Amanda further details some of the specific items of clothing that in Durban signify a coloured boy:

> He'll either wear Levis, or Collies or Dickies, instead of wearing our school pants, it's like a lighter shade. Instead of wearing government gray, as they put it . . . . Shoes you'd see a lot of the coloured boys wear—All-Stars, Converse, Nike, Reebok, Sebagos, like that.

Sebago shoes are the most popular footwear, followed by Nikes. Levis jeans are an obsession with coloured students, and the combination of Sebagos and Levis, or Sebagos and Dickies (a chino-style type pant) is a definite and clear marker of a coloured youth. Short-sleeved checked shirts are another common item (predominantly among girls), as are baseball warmup jackets. These distinctions are well known to Fernwood students of all races. Octavia, an African student, comments on coloured dress, ". . . they wear Dickies trousers, All Star takkies [sneakers], they wear Converse takkies, they wear like these checked shirts."

Coloured taste is largely determined by boys, with girls closely following their lead. Amanda comments on this phenomenon, "The girls, a lot of them, also go wear Levis jeans . . . a lot of the coloured girls actually dress up like boys. Myself, I own a very few skirts and dresses, it's mostly pants, jeans, shirts." Diane, an Indian girl who follows coloured style similarly remarked, "We like checked skirts, Dickies and Levis. More casual." Amanda and Diane's observations are continually verified through my own: weekends and holidays spent watching coloured girls in town, at the disco, and at the mall reveal that their choice of clothing both falls, almost always, within the very narrow limits described above and carefully conceals sexuality in a way that is markedly different from white girls', as I will discuss later in this section.

In contrast to coloured students, African students at Fernwood blend and mix the influences of African-American hip-hop culture, and, particularly for the girls, more expensive European fashion. Thobile, an African girl, comments that the boys at the multiracial schools tend to be more influenced by American style than boys at township schools: ". . . they just have their style. Even the way they dress, they like wearing jeans, big baggy jeans, and Bomba takkies, and big t-shirts. They sort of adopt black American style." But for African students, the overriding concern is not to look American, but to look "smart." This obsession with looking sharp and well dressed is often invoked to mark the differences between African and white students. African girls often prefer more expensive and elegant clothing than coloured girls, wearing silk shirts paired with high priced jeans and gold jewelry. A white girl, Jill, notes that this is a major dividing factor between white and African girls:

> Often we'll find that whites will go out, and they won't even buy something, they'll just pull out something from their cupboard and they just slap it on . . . They [Africans] wear very fancy clothes. Silk pants and silk tops, that's what we've often found. The girls mainly. Boys wear jeans, baggy jeans, and t-shirts generally, or baggy button-up shirts.

For African girls, being stylish and smart is very important—a quality that some, including Amanda, a coloured girl, admire. She remembers, "The fashion show is an example. When the African girls came to watch, they didn't just come in anything. They usually make a statement without saying a word."

Price is an overriding consideration for African students. While labels are extremely important to coloured students and these items are expensive in South African terms, there is a ceiling. For example, a coloured student's preferences in jeans is Levis only—wearing more expensive jeans will not elevate social status, only the label "Levis" will. For African students, however, social status is intimately connected to the price one pays for a particular commodity. African students are more likely than coloureds to bypass American jeans and identification, instead preferring European names such as Giorgio Armani and Daniel Hechter. Zola, an African girl, comments on this phenomenon, explaining that whites don't dress in style, and

> buy jeans that are R50 [7] or something. But when you are black [African], you are wearing R50 jeans, people are going to say mmm, that's ugly. We are looking for labels and names. We just look for the label, and the label counts, and it costs as well.

Although there are some lines of continuity between coloured, African, and Indian styles, white students inhabit a completely distinct fashion universe, one that is influenced by both surfer and rave cultures. White students often spend their weekends at the beach in downtown Durban, and their shorts, sandals, and torn T-shirts reflect their casual style. With a few exceptions, whites are unconcerned about labels and price, buying relatively cheap clothes that coloured and African students would consider sloppy and unfashionable. Whites' attire in the evenings is strongly linked to their participation in rave culture, and they usually wear the bright, garish, fluorescent clothing associated with raving. Again, the lines that separate black and white are well known by all students. Rena, a coloured student, talks about respecting different styles in a way that is reminiscent of discourses of cultural tolerance, "We have to respect the different kinds of clothes, and we wear Levis and checked shirts, and they wear rave clothes." Peter, a white boy, similarly observes, "Talking about different races, the coloureds and the blacks dress smart when they go out, they've got their longs on. The whites they wear what we call rave clothes."

White girls dress in a style that emphasizes their sexuality more than coloured and African girls. Jill relates, "Often the girls wear short wrap skirts, and then tight tops. And you normally wear a top with a saying on it, like 'babe' or 'angel' or something like that." Amanda also notes the differences between white and coloured taste:

> With the white girls, like Vicki, we went out one day, and we agreed to wear black leather skirts. Her skirt was sitting up here [gestures towards the upper thigh], and my skirt was sitting down there [gestures lower on the thigh].So we just dress differently. We do everything differently.

While white girls feel comfortable displaying their sexuality, African and coloured girls are considerably more cautious. Coloured girls in particular rarely wear clothing that would be considered feminine or sexual—the perceived risks of harassment and violence are too great. White girls' increased comfort may be related to the fact that, in general, they live in residential areas that are easier to get to and safer than those of coloured and African girls, and they have greater access to private transportation. In contrast, African and coloured girls often must cross treacherous terrain (especially at night) to travel to and from home: for example, they often have to go into town and wait at a taxi rank and then walk through unsafe streets when they arrive in their neighborhood. White girls are more likely to get rides with parents or friends into town, or to frequent clubs in the suburbs, thus avoiding placing their bodies in a vulnerable position in a dangerous part of the city.

For all students, fashion works to suture racial identities around particular taste practices. Taste becomes a substantive, generative part of the creation of racialized identities.

DIVISIONS ON THE DANCE FLOOR

Like clothing, musical taste is linked to collective, racialized identities. In general terms, most Fernwood students would agree that Africans listen to rhythm and blues, "slow" music such as Whitney Houston, some rap, and what is known as "local" music, which is sometimes sung in Zulu, sometimes in English, or a combination of the two. Coloured students' (and in this case, coloureds' and Indians' taste differs) musical tastes are similar to Africans, except for the absence of local music. White music takes several trajectories, and includes rave, heavy metal, "mellow" music like the Cranberries, and for a small minority of white students, gangsta rap. As mentioned previously there are very few Indian students at Fernwood, yet Indians are usually described as liking techno, pop, and rhythm and blues, thus showing signs of mixing music from genres that are generally regarded as separate.

The racial division of music is well known to the majority of Fernwood students. Many teachers, however, are uninformed about the sharp divides regarding musical taste. For example, in one English class I observed on a regular basis the teacher used an Alanis Morrisette song to illustrate the concept of irony for her class, which is over 90% African. Although the teacher thought she was connecting to her students through using popular music, the class overwhelmingly did not know Alanis Morrisette or simply dismissed her song as white music. Students, in contrast, are acutely aware of the racial borders and boundaries of music. Jackie, a white girl, comments, "They [coloureds and Africans] listen more to lovey, dovey, and I think you're so beautiful and please have sex with me." Marlene, an Indian student, remarked about rhythm and blues, "It's mostly the coloureds and the blacks, some blacks. And mostly the white children like Nirvana and Metallica and stuff like that. It's not that I'm racist or anything, it's just that I don't like it. It's noise." In this case, Marlene, an extremely polite and respectful student, is apologetic that she does not like what is termed white music. Accepting music as a basis for difference, she is quick to add that she is not racist. Debra, an African girl, told me about her friendship with a white girl and the way that music became an area of difference and tension:

> Like she likes this music, this heavy metal music, and like I told you I like r and b. She did like r and b, but not as much as I do. I couldn't handle it, that was the worst thing I couldn't handle. I would come to her house and she would play it, and I would say Nicole I don't like it, and she played it. I just couldn't handle it.

Peter, a white boy, succinctly describes the differences, "You got the black race that likes jazz, and then the whites go for either heavy metal, techno, trance, pump . . . the coloureds go for slow songs, like Nikki goes for all these nice slow songs like Kenny G."

For many students, like Dumisani, musical taste is seen as unchanging:

> Our music is not the same as most of the white people. Most of the white people listen to like rock, and heavy metal, and their music, but we don't listen to them, and there's nothing you can do about that. That's just the way it is.

Samantha, a white girl, makes a similar comment about a classmate of hers, who is African. "Like Thandeka, she wouldn't like to come, say to a nightclub with us, because her music's different. She's got different ways of doing things." For many students, despite a shift to a discourse of taste to describe difference, taste is still as fixed, inscribed, and immobilized as biology. Difference in musical taste can also be framed as the primary mark of cultural difference. Elaine, an Indian girl, talks about dating white boys: "I have been dating white guys, and they're fine. I don't see any difference except for cultural background." When I asked her what she meant by "cultural background," Elaine replies, "There's a type of music he likes, and that I like, and it's really different. He liked going out to certain places, like loud places, and I like going out somewhere else." In some cases, different tastes in music are given as a legitimate reason for the continued separation of whites and blacks. Nikki, a coloured student, remarks:

> I asked Octavia how she would feel if a coloured person moved into a black area, and she said it was okay, because we all listen to the same music. But you

> [Nadine] would listen to different music, if you were a white from here . . . .
> you'd listen to different music, you'd buy different clothes. That's why you
> wouldn't be comfortable.

In this case, Nikki and Octavia agree that mixing between coloureds and
Africans is acceptable because of (some) shared musical tastes, but that whites'
tastes are fundamentally incompatible, and thus they must be geographically
separate. In another instance, Janice, a white student, uses music to justify the
social segregation of Africans and whites:

> I prefer the blacks [Africans] being at their own club, because I don't like the
> kind of dancing that they do. They go out and listen to their beat, dance side
> to side. We dance to techno like this [demonstrates, moving up and down].
> But they do hey, hey, and they're all in a big circle and they look like they're
> having a toyi-toyi [8] session. And you can't do that in the middle of the club,
> I mean, you can't leave a space in the middle . . . . Have you ever been to Red
> Dog [a white club in town]? Red Dog is squashed, you are squashed, you have
> no chance to go hey, hey, and do this funny dance.

From Janice's perspective, the style of dance associated with a particular type of
music is problematic, creating a justification for social segregation. In these
instances, music is being used to mark fundamental differences: to map out territory that is racially bounded. These dynamics of separation play themselves
out as musical taste takes center stage during school functions, such as the school
fashion show and matric dance.

Defining Self and Other: The Public Marking of Difference

At many Model C high schools in Durban, school fashion shows are annual traditions. Less effort than a school play or musical, fashion shows allow students to
momentarily live and experience a glamorous world. Fashion shows, of course,
have no plot, so there are no lines to learn or characters to develop. There is simply clothing and music, and thus they become the critical sites of struggle for students. The Fernwood fashion show takes place early in the year, and rehearsals are
already under way when I arrive at the school a few weeks after the official beginning of the year. Trouble, however, has already erupted, as the cast of the fashion
show threatens a strike. As I was to learn later, even the threat of a strike was significant as no one could remember Fernwood students ever before contemplating
such an action. The administration quickly quashes the strike by calling a mandatory cast meeting, and as the dynamics of the now cancelled strike unfold during
the meeting, it becomes clear that the planned strike has clear racial dynamics.
The leaders of the strike, a group of white girls, have two sets of complaints that
encompass both the local racial politics of Fernwood and a larger set of global cultural politics. First, white students are unhappy because the previous week the
administration had taken control of the fashion show away from the students and

brought in a local professional who had volunteered his time to direct the production. As Michael Green explains to me, the white students in charge of the production are disorganized and furthermore insisted on casting only their friends in most scenes, relegating the black students to small and peripheral roles. The white students are upset—they are no longer in charge.

But this local play of racial politics is complicated by a larger, looming factor: the choice of music for the fashion show. The white students insist that the music be exclusively techno music, which they, and others, consistently identify as music that signifies white identity. The issue of the choice of music, more than the issue of control, was to be the pre-eminent issue of the strike. Although there are black students in the fashion, show it seems that few of them are prepared to strike, and furthermore they do not support the premise of the strike—that only techno music should be used in the fashion show. Most of the black students are content with the current mix of techno, pop, rap, and children's songs.

For the white students, however, the music of the fashion show becomes synonymous with control of the space and projection of an identity that is grounded in a whiteness centered in techno music. Taste categories, here techno music, are the predominant way that white students define, project, and enact their racialized identity. The whiteness they construct is not tied to cultural markers that rest on South African soil. Students are not insisting on the inclusion of cultural markers of apartheid-era nationalism or even what might be described as a more generalized South African white culture. Instead, students cling to the styles and tastes of global whiteness, here specifically music, to consolidate an identity about that they feel and express passionate attachments. This "global whiteness" has its roots in popular culture and functions as a scape that binds, however unevenly, white youth around the world through the cultural practice of techno music. It matters little that the "roots" of techno music are to be found in the African-American community in Detroit (Cooper, Knuckles, moby, Owen, & Ross, 1995), as a genre, techno music operates globally as music associated with white youth, who have resituated its roots in various European countries. At Fernwood, taste works to produce and reproduce racial difference, and the explosive politics that emerge over the fashion show demonstrate how critical it is to students' sense of racialized selves.

There are also occasions when the combination of local and global racial politics divides students who are trying to come together. While grade 11 students traditionally plan the official matric (senior class) dance, the afterparty is wholly controlled by the graduating students. For many students the afterparty is even more important than the school-sponsored function, and some students skip the dance and just attend the afterparty. Traditionally, one afterparty is held for the entire senior class, either at someone's house, a local hotel, or other public venue.

But this year there is difficulty. Discussions of possible locations for the afterparty begin in May and continue through mid-July, the week of the dance. A small group of grade 12 girls, who take on the responsibility of finding a place to hold

the party, continually confront the racial borders of Durban and of popular culture. At first a solution appears to be found, as one white girl offers her house for
the party. But many of the black students are uncomfortable going to her neighborhood and the idea is rejected. Similarly, white students will not go to parties
in black areas, so private homes are abandoned and the focus turns to clubs. But
problems arise there too. Black students refuse to go to clubs that play white music,
and white students refuse to go to coloured or Indian clubs. Other venues are considered but the local politics of safety and comfort in various neighborhoods combined with the racial taste politics of music make every location untenable.
Charles, a coloured student, comments on the problem facing the senior class:

> On a night like the matric ball it's the one and only night you want to be free
> to do what you like. Now if you go to a place like Addington Beach, it's in a
> white area, it's a white beach, it was for whites down the years, blacks
> [Africans] wouldn't feel comfortable there. They probably would get remarks
> from whites, not from schoolmates, but from outsiders. Then if you go to a
> place like the Village Green, where the blacks congregate and stuff by the mil-
> lions, whites wouldn't feel comfortable. So it's quite a tricky decision where
> to go. And also the safety of the pupils.

The issue remains unresolved up to and including the night of the matric dance
as it becomes apparent that the Fernwood tradition of one afterparty will finally
collapse—unable to find common ground. Unity, even a patched-together, unstable, rocky unity, eludes them. While the remnants of apartheid Durban certainly
provide one strong factor in this scenario, it is not the only one: The divides produced through the racial politics of music also contribute to the ultimate fractur-
ing of the matric class on its last night together.

THE FORCE OF TASTE

Taste, as Chris Richards (1999) notes, is often a way that youth mark and define
friendship. As he writes,

> subjects may position themselves in relations with others through a mapping
> of such relations onto the allegiances and divisions available in discursively
> constructed taste categories: friends might, for example, register "friendship"
> through a common liking for rap and not pop. (p. 256)

But within the confines of Fernwood, and situated within the context of racial
tension and conflict, taste becomes more than a marker of friendship and com-
patibility—it becomes the primary signifier and practice of race. Discourses of
culture, history, and biology no longer suffice to explain racial difference.
Unable to build a racial identity solely around these aging signifiers, students
look for other ways—other methods—of defining who they are in relation to
those who are racially different; race is recoded. They turn to the world of fash-

ion and music, and a discourse of taste, to ground and explain the persistence of separation.

The racialized discourse of taste transpires in a global arena, but one that is significantly changed from that of the teachers. While the teachers' globality (discussed in chapter 4) reflects a colonial, modernist picture of the world, students' racialized selves are constructed in an increasingly postmodern one. The commodities that signify African, coloured, Indian, and white are picked out from global circulation, and then deployed within the site of the school to mark race. Many of these commodities, like Levis, Sebagos, Nikes, and Reeboks do not have the same connotations (racial or otherwise) in New York or London. A Fernwood student might be shocked, for example, to visit the United States and find some whites wearing Levis and Reeboks, and some blacks wearing inexpensive no-name jeans. Global commodities, in this case, take on meanings that are specifically local and not therefore transferable to other nations or cities. It is also significant that almost none of these commodities have their origins in South Africa; they are not produced by nor do they reflect indigenous, settler, or national cultures in an unproblematic or simple way. In most cases, their lines of origin are nonexistent. Students do not, and cannot, say that these commodities have populated their families' lives in recent generations or historically. Instead, these commodities are produced by transnational corporations and marketed to youth worldwide who use symbolic creativity to transform them into products and symbols that are meaningful within particular local contexts.

Race's significance in a moment of national and, arguably, global, transformation is not necessarily diminished. Yet it does not, and cannot, function in exactly the same manner that it did for previous generations. Changing circumstances guarantee that race—as a source of identification, as a political entity, as a social reality—will not remain stagnant. As it is reconstituted through taste, race takes on contradictory impulses—at once to reproduce itself and to break free. These divergent forces are taken up in the following chapter.

CHAPTER SIX

BORDERWORK:

CONFLICT AND CONNECTION

At Fernwood, taste operates as an integral aspect of the formation and exercise of racialized identities. Taste does not exist as a backdrop to the racial relations that unfold; its dynamics, in part, help to produce those relations. This chapter looks at two forces in the racial relations at Fernwood, those of conflict and connection, and weaves together a discussion that encompasses multiple dynamics, including that of taste. Although race is reproduced, it is simultaneously recast, giving rise to both moments and spaces of conflict, and equally salient spaces of connection. In these ways, students work the borders, or what Gloria Anzaldúa (1987; Anzaldúa & Hernandez, 1996) refers to as the "Borderlands." She writes: "...the Borderlands are present wherever two or more cultures edge each other, where people of different races occupy the same territory, where under, lower, middle and upper classes touch, where the space between two individuals shrinks with intimacy" (preface). I use the idea of Borderlands not to posit the borders as naturally occurring demarcations between races and cultures, but as an effect of the "enunciation of difference" (Scott, 1995). The space in between is also, as Anzaldúa argues, a place of "hatred, anger and exploitation." Those who exist in or encounter these borders, including the students at Fernwood, collide and connect, as they remap identities within these spaces.

Racialized conflict is endemic, but plays itself out through practices that go beyond the schoolyard fight or the racial slur. Instead, it is also embedded in the politics of taste, specifically the policing of racial taste borders and the resentment of whites towards black students. Connections, which are more difficult to access, are also tied up in the racial politics of taste, among other factors. To illustrate the dynamic of connection, I tell two stories: that of alliances between African and coloured girls in the matric class, and of coloured, white, and Indian students in the younger grades (predominantly grade 8). Connections are not stable, but shift between the older and younger levels of the school.

Within both connection and conflict, class begins to emerge as part of the story of racialized identities and taste. Class clearly does not function in a unitary manner at Fernwood. For example, poor white and black students, though sometimes of a relatively similar class background, are polarized and frequently hostile. Many students (though certainly more whites than blacks) would recoil at the thought of any shared economic or political interest. The class dynamics of South Africa have been historically so saturated with race that this is a predictable phenomenon. Thus, within Fernwood, taste is not formative of class relations to the same extent that it influences racialized identities, positions, and alliances. Fernwood students do not deliberately and methodically set out to produce class-differentiated identities, though their racialized identities are, in many ways, shot through with class dynamics. Although class plays a secondary role in this book, which primarily focuses on race, it is still an influential element in the dynamics of racial relations at Fernwood.

CONFLICT

Daily life at Fernwood, as discussed in chapter 3, is saturated with racial conflict. Even on your first visit to Fernwood, you would undoubtedly notice the racial divides on the field before school and during the two daily breaks. Simphiwe, an African student, jokingly refers to this practice as the "Group Areas Act" [1]—a holdover from apartheid. He explains, "During the school's lunch and tea breaks you will see one group of blacks there, one group of whites, one group of coloureds, and one group of Asians over there." Certain areas of the field are often recognized as the "turf" of a particular racial group (and often a subset thereof), despite the management's (very limited) attempts to prevent this practice. Aside from the occasional fights, the different racial groups at Fernwood often appear to have little daily contact. While racial epithets are frequent, in classrooms and hallways, many times the racial groups at Fernwood seem to simply go their own way: coexisting in time and space, but not communicating. Maureen sees this phenomenon as inevitable, "But trying to bring us together or trying to force us together is not going to help because we'll still just go our own separate ways." As Maureen suggests, in many corners of Fernwood, a stony, hostile silence prevails punctuated by fiery though short-lived flare-ups of racial antagonism.

While overt hostility may be on the wane, the constancy of race is unabating. It is present in virtually every interaction, around every corner, underlying every moment of the day. Though Fernwood students may, on the surface, appear to be ignoring (or, on a good day, tolerating) those who are racial "others," they are actually furiously working to ensure that race persists.

POLICING RACIAL BORDERS

The racial borders of taste, described in chapter 5, are not voluntarily codes. Instead, they are actively policed, as a way of trying to ensure that difference is maintained. Collective, racialized identities become paramount, as individual students who breach racial norms are ostracized. Jill, a white girl, relates what happens to an African girl who shows up at school on a civvies day in clothing that is perceived as white:

> Last year we had a civvies day, I think for Valentine's Day, and this one black [African] girl came to school in tights and a baggy top, and she was laughed at. It was so funny, it was like the whole school burst into this laughing stock, and none of us could figure out why . . . . We spoke to some of them, and they said you can't just like rock up [show up] in tights like that. But we all said, you wear them around the house, it's just civvies day, it's not like you're in a fashion parade.

In this example, African students collectively impose racialized taste norms on a student who wears clothing that is perceived as white. Octovia, an African student, explains the taste codes that govern her selection of jewelry and accessories, "…they [white people] can even wear silver, it doesn't matter. But for us I wouldn't wear silver even if I was caught dead. It's not really culture, it's fashion, but for us, fashion, we like to be flashy, to wear gold." A similar dynamic operates among other groups, as Tanya and Muriel, two coloured students, relate,

> Tanya: Like we've got a style of dressing, and every coloured wants to conform to that style of dressing. But I want to be unique, and the minute you are different . . . .
>
> Muriel: You're persecuted.

Muriel goes on to explain how her coloured peers reject her because of her taste in music:

> You see me I'm a coloured, but I love white people, the way white people sing, like Alanis Morrisette. I like her, I don't love her. But when I tell my friends I like Alanis Morrisette, they tell me I'm sick and all that. But I'm a person who likes a whole range of things. I don't like to conform to one thing. They tell me I'm sick and all that, and go away.

Despite the expense involved with purchasing clothing, particularly for coloured and African students, students know that they will encounter ridicule and rejection if they wear the "wrong" clothing. This does not mean, of course, that every single student at Fernwood conforms to the dictates of their collective racialized selves. First, as I will discuss in the next chapter, there are students who resist the imposition of taste norms. Second, there are undoubtedly others whose families simply cannot afford the "right" clothing. Although these students lack access to the commodities that mark their racialized selves, they still must operate within a universe in which taste solidifies race. This reality, of course, is not limited to the space of the school, but also extends to other areas of Durban, particularly town. Molefe, an African student, observes:

> You wouldn't find a black [African] person go to town . . . . a very much huge majority, you wouldn't find them wearing shorts to town. They always wear long pants, always trying to look smart and buy expensive clothes. And you find most of the whites, as I said they are much open, they don't really care what other people have to say . . . . Black people we are concerned about what other people are going to say.

Molefe may underestimate how much white youth care about what others say (for white students do and would surely talk if a white adopted African, coloured, or Indian taste codes), yet he pinpoints the strictures felt by African students, who understand that racial solidarity is lived, in part, through clothing.

The collective imposition of racialized taste codes at Fernwood ensures that division and conflict persist. Despite the financial and personal strain of maintaining these taste borders, it becomes difficult, if not impossible, for most students to step outside them. Taste, in this instance, is reproductive of racialized identities that are derivative of, though not identical to, the racialized identities of apartheid. For white students, as I detail in the following section, taste plays a prominent role in the emergent politics of resentment.

THE POLITICS OF WHITE RESENTMENT

The politics of taste also serves as a springboard for white resentment, which further fuels racial antagonism. Through the practices of resentment, white students at Fernwood construct identities through the "strategy of negating the other and the tactical and strategic deployment of moral evaluation and emotion"(McCarthy et al., 1997, p. 84). Clothing, and on occasion music, are sites in which white students express growing anger about their increasingly marginalized (at least from their perspective) position at Fernwood, and more generally in South Africa. Janice, a white girl, comments on the music and fashion preferences of African students:

> If they are in the shop, and they hear music playing, they'll just start their little dances in the shop there, and I find that very uncultured, you're in public . . . . Another thing, if you are going to the beach for the day, and they wear their long, smart pants and their silk tops, and their fancy shoes, instead of

takkies [sneakers], baggies, t-shirts. That's what irritates me. Whites wear what
is comfortable, they always dress up smart, smart, smart. If you look on break-
up day, if we still had civvies on break-up [last day of school] day, you would
be hysterical. One girl came in a bridesmaid's dress last year. [*Nadine:* Why's
that?]. I've got no clue. I think they are trying to act better than whites. I don't
think they are purposely trying to do it, but in their subconscious they are.

Here, clothing takes on very specific and charged race and class connotations. Janice invokes a discourse of primitiveness to describe African students' ways of dancing, so as to confirm white superiority. Janice frames her unease through a discourse of taste that quickly turns into an assertion of racial superiority. She moves
rapidly from expressing irritation at African students' clothing choices, to charg-
ing them with "trying to act better than whites," a scenario that clearly makes her
uncomfortable as it reverses her naturalized racial assumptions.

Other white students, who are perhaps a bit less hostile, also express puz-
zlement over African students' choices of clothing and, again, blend comments
about their classmates' clothing with their perception that whites are in a disad-
vantaged position in post-apartheid South Africa. For example, Rosa comments:

We have civvies day at school, and you notice the white people come in baggies and t-shirts, but the black pupils get dressed up in nice larny pants, nice
shoes, they think they're going to some fancy party instead of civvies day.

Later on in our conversation, Rosa adds, "The only thing that I can know that's
changed is about the jobs now. The blacks can go in first, and the whites get taken
afterward . . . . I just think that's very wrong." These two statements encompass
most of what Rosa claims she knows about Africans, marking complementary ways
in which she feels displaced in South Africa as a white. Blacks are asserting their
presence both through control of the job market and through their choice of clothing, which is fancier than that preferred by whites. Kevin, a white boy, similarly
remarks that "I don't go for brands, they are so expensive," a reality that separates
him from many of his black classmates. Like Janice, Rosa's racial antagonism and
Kevin's resignation is expressed through a discourse of taste, and is intimately
linked to their unease over the shifting of what they had assumed were naturalized and enduring class positions.

Sometimes other commodities become a site for this resentment. For example, Mark tells me about the "Indian guy who lives next door and has six Mer-
cedes." and Theresa observes that she has on multiple occasions seen BMWs at
squatter camps:

Theresa:	Not everyone's got the money to live in a proper house. Like some squatters drive around in BMWs.
Nadine:	Do you know squatters who have BMWs?
Theresa:	No, but you go by the squatter camps and there are BMWs parked outside.

Nadine: How do you think that happens?
Theresa: They don't pay for rent or nothing.

Theresa seems to believe that living in a squatter camp is simply a lifestyle choice, thus allowing one to own a BMW, which is a luxury her family could never afford. While it is of course far-fetched to assume that many (if any!) squatters own BMWs, Theresa's assertion about the purchasing power and economic status of even the poorest of the poor in Durban speaks to her feeling that every black person is more privileged than she. Yet she also finds a way to "explain" this privilege—squatters don't pay rent—and thus hangs on to her sense that she is still, really, better than a squatter (her family pays a rent/mortgage and thus can't afford a BMW). In a similar vein, when I ask Jackie, a white student, what is the most confusing or difficult thing about living in South Africa, she replies:

> Looking at a really, really interesting car, and thinking, geez, it's so cool, and looking inside the tinted windows, and it's hard to get used to seeing so many black people now having big cars, now having good clothing. It's just nothing we've seen before. In some ways, there were some black people that did have nice things, but they were higher in government, and you saw them now and again.

Although previously black wealth was contained and explained through positions in government, its sudden availability to a larger (though, in actuality, still miniscule) number of Africans is unsettling for Jackie.

Running through it all is the white fear of marginalization and the sense that this generation is being forced to compensate blacks for past mistreatment. As Ben writes with exasperation:

> Why do sports teams have to have Africans in them, why do Africans have to be made leaders? They should not get the position because they have the right skin colour, it should be because they deserve it. It also makes me angry when Africans throw the struggle up into everybody's face; yes, it was sad, but it's over now, leave it where it belongs—in the past.

Music, fashion, and other commodities function to fuel white resentment, as hostility over black (here specifically African) taste categories merges with white fears about their prospects for jobs and a financially secure future in South Africa. Thus, the borders that cause conflict at Fernwood are overtly racial, but also overlaid with the dynamics of class conflict, as pockets of middle-class blacks meet working-class whites. This phenomenon is particularly strong in the matric class, because, as discussed in chapter 3, Fernwood's older black student population in 1996 is more heavily middle-class than in the younger grades. White, working-class Fernwood students, who previously enjoyed advantages because of their white status, find themselves losing their grip on control of the school and their futures in South Africa. White students can no longer easily dismiss blacks as primitive, less modern, or less intelligent, though, as I have noted, some of those discourses linger. Instead, white students now confront black students within a different context and lash out at black students who they now perceive have nicer clothes, fancier cars, and more promising lives. Taste becomes the ground not just for marking racial difference, but for perpetuating racial hatred, though in a new context in which whites command less political power, and somewhat decreasing (though still obviously overwhelming) economic power. White students are outnumbered, and tend to avoid (with some exceptions) direct conflict with black students. Yet the politics of resentment and its effects fester, exacerbating the recreation of racialized identities and promoting racial conflict

CONNECTING ACROSS BORDERS

While conflict and division dominate the racial relations at Fernwood, they are not the sole dynamic. In smaller spaces between individuals and small groups, in brief moments and slight but sustained patterns, there are breaks that reveal that the story is more intricate and nuanced than one of strife and schism. What emerges in these fleeting moments and spaces are connections—often uneven, never perfectly harmonious, but moments nonetheless when ties and bonds are forged.

Students who express the desire to connect with individuals from other racial groups often see music, particularly clubs, as the place where the crossover would occur. For example, Rosa, a white student, considers the possibility of going to a coloured club: "I know there is a club in town where they [coloured students] go, Zoom or something. Melissa says I must come with them one night to the club. I'm getting up the courage to do that. Check it out, see what it's like." Another student, Octavia, who is African, acknowledges that both taste differences and local racial realities keep her from joining white students at their club:

> I can't really go to club 330 because they don't play my type of music. Even if it were my type of music, you'd find people there who are anti-black, who'd try to hurt me. So rather me not go there, than going to a club where I'm not protected.

Although there are fleeting impulses to experience the social space of other racial groups, crossings are viewed as dangerous, both because of the violation of racial norms and the potential physical danger. But as Lipsitz (1994) comments, music opens the possibilities for many varieties of "dangerous crossroads", where connections can be formed that would otherwise be unthinkable and largely unavailable. In the balance of this section I will discuss two spaces that constitute the "dangerous crossroads" at Fernwood High, and draw attention to how popular culture works in concert with local dynamics to create, sustain, and break racial alliances.

CROSSROADS I: AFRICANS, COLOUREDS, AND THE PRACTICE OF RACIALIZED TEASING

"Didn't you hear me, I said no kaffirs [2] over here"; "You coloureds, you're raw, you got no culture"; "Okay, Miss sexy legs Bombay, go back to India"; "Ahh, go back to the bush!" Racial insults fly thick and fast across the room, as Mr. du Plessis' class settles in for English. Mr. du Plessis and other teachers overhear these comments daily; they are part of the regular routine of relations between particular groups of students at Fernwood. There is no sense that this behavior is unacceptable; not once did I hear a teacher interrupt or challenge these comments. When I first arrived at Fernwood I was puzzled by this behavior—did these racial slurs actually express hostility, were students simply mimicking what they learned as children, or were other dynamics also involved?

These racial slurs are regularly exchanged by a group of coloured and African girls. One of the coloured girls is half-Indian, which prompts the calls for her to go back to India. The dynamics between these African and coloured students at Fernwood encompass both racial intolerance and points of acceptance and genuine friendship. Several factors structure their relations: patterns of desegregation at Fernwood; class dynamics, and, of particular interest here, practices including, but in this case, not limited to, those grounded in popular culture. The observations and analysis I make here in "Crossroads I" are restricted to relations between African and coloured students at the senior level only. As will become clear through this section and the next (Crossroads II), points of racial connection shift within Fernwood.

The matric (senior) class at Fernwood is 50% white, though that percentage drops sharply down through the grades. A significant portion of the African students and almost all the coloured students in the senior class have spent their entire high school career at Fernwood. Many entered an all-white school in 1991 and experienced its transformation into a school that is now predominantly African. In the early years these African and coloured students were greatly outnumbered, and bonds have been created as they came together to confront a majority white, and not necessarily welcoming, school. In addition, many coloured and African students share a relatively similar class background at the matric level: few are very poor, most are from working-class and lower middle-class backgrounds. African and coloured students at this level come together primarily because of a shared racial experience at Fernwood, but their class similarity helps to shore up their relationship.

Although these local factors allow African and coloured matric students to see each other as allies, music cements these relations on a daily, lived basis. As I noted in a slightly different context in chapter 5, Nikki, a coloured student, tells me, "I asked Octavia [who is African] how she would feel if a coloured person moved into a black [African] area, and she said it was okay, because we all listen to the same music." Here Nikki, Octavia, and other students use similar musical taste (for rhythm and blues, female vocalists such as Whitney Houston, and some rap) as a way of understanding and accepting the links that they see between coloured and African students. Popular culture, instead of other dynamics, such as politics, history, or even family ties, becomes the ground on which affiliation is built and maintained. Dumisani, an African student, comments, "Our [African] parties are more like coloured parties. The white parties are different because you have to get into the music." Thobile, an African girl, adds, "So some of them [coloureds] fall into the white group, and some of them just hold on to black people, because most coloureds, normally, they are for blacks." These connections among African and coloured students in the matric class are firmed up early in the year, as Fernwood sponsors its first Debs' ball. A tradition in Indian and coloured (but not white) schools in the Durban area, girls in grades 11 and 12 who wish to be Debs fundraise for the school for months before the event. Amanda, the Fernwood head girl and of mixed coloured and Indian descent, spearheads the drive to bring a Debs' ball to the school. The planning and organization of the dance is controlled by African, Indian, and coloured students—white students are noticeably absent from this major school event. Given the historical trajectory of the Debs' ball, and the local leadership at the school, white students in general stay away, and the event becomes an occasion for older (only grade 11 and 12 students are allowed to attend), primarily black Fernwood students to create ties through a shared experience. With black students in control of the music, Whitney Houston and rhythm and blues dominate, and the dance floor is crowded with black students, asserting their presence at and ownership of their school dance. Despite these intense moments of connection, relations are still governed by lingering racism, particularly on the part of coloured students. For example, Melissa, a coloured student, comments, "Some of the whites still don't like the blacks [Africans], they pretend to not be racist. Everyone is kind of racist to me, and I'm a bit racist." The racialized teasing discussed previously expresses the ambivalent relations between these coloured and African girls, at once united and separated. White students rarely participate in these exchanges, though they are often silent witnesses. Nikki, a coloured student who is a member of this group, again comments on the racial dynamics:

> We tease each other all the time. We tell the blacks [Africans] to go back to the jungle, they call us zebras. We leave the white children out because they can't take a joke and that kind of thing. They get all excited and upset about it and we basically don't interact with them that much. I mean there are a few that I hang around with, but the majority of them, trust me, I don't like.

The casualness and consistency with which coloureds and Africans tease each other about their racial identities demonstrate the ties that keep them together in a school that is still dominated, symbolically and materially, by whites. It is a game that white students cannot join in the current climate because they are afraid of being accused of being racist. When I ask Janice, a white girl, what she has learned about other races that she did not know before attending Fernwood she replies:

To be very careful how you insult them when you are joking with them. I mean, Melissa can take me to the office for calling her a coolie, [3] and Marissa can take me to the office for calling her a stupid kaffir. But let them call me anything, I can't do anything about it.

Janice watches the interaction of the coloured and African girls everyday and in fact invokes their practice of teasing to demonstrate that she too can be an insider:

It's nice, we get on with the black [African] people, we tell them to go back to the bush and all that. We have fun. It's much better to me. If I was in a white school I'd be going on and I'd be calling them all kaffirs in the street and getting myself killed. So in this school it's nice. Numbuso I say, you stupid kaffir, come here and I joke with her.

But Janice's ability to enter that circle is limited—her joking interactions with Numbuso are rare and don't exhibit the depth of connection (though conflicted) that exists between the coloured and African girls. Coloured and African students take center stage as they enter Mr. du Plessis' English class, as a group seizing space and attention that would otherwise probably revert to the white students, who number about 50% of the class. Publicly, they solidify their bonds, letting white students know that they are united and, as proof, they demonstrate that they can participate in this practice from which white students are excluded. A shared taste in music both strengthens these bonds and creates an explanation, in the eyes of white students, for the connections that exist between Africans and coloureds.

But the practices of racialized teasing also reveal the ongoing tensions that coloured and African students feel—their lack of comfort with each other, their distrust, the ongoing racism that exists. As I spent a good percentage of my time with the matrics, the constant (between every class period, at break, at the beginning of every class, at every opportunity) racial teasing became quite repetitive, wearing, and finally annoying. I began to wonder about the relationships between these girls: Do their ties actually go beyond the exchange of loud, persistent racial insults? I was searching for evidence of positive relations between them, which many of them had talked about in interviews, but I had failed to see materialize in my presence.

Then one day towards the end of the year, Mr. du Plessis is called away and the class is sent down the hall to Elizabeth Ashby's classroom, where she would supervise them for the period. Many of the students know Mrs. Ashby and they like and respect her. Their behavior changes as soon as they walk into Mrs. Ashby's classroom: from the loud, boisterous girls always arguing with Mr. du Plessis, to quieter, more respectful students. Mr. du Plessis has left assigned work for them to do, but it is universally ignored. Instead, the regular group of African and coloured girls gather in the back of the class together—white students are scattered in small groups throughout the class, as are the few African boys who in general had little connection with the girls' group. It is towards the end of the year and many of the girls have with them photo albums of themselves as children. Photos are passed around, everyone laughing and commenting on each other's clothes and hair and remembering their childhood. The constant edge that frames their interactions seems to drift away at least momentarily. The omnipresent barrier of race wanes as they find common ground in their memories: battling with their mothers over their hair, refusing to wear certain items of clothing, and suffering from their mothers' collective bad taste in toddler attire. The connections between them that are usually unspoken become tangible as conflict gives way. The bonds between these girls are certainly uneven: Race is not ignored or transcended. But it is actively struggled with—the girls, for a moment, seeing each other as friends.

But the public bonds displayed in Mrs. Ashby's class are only forged between the African and coloured girls—the white girls stand outside and apart from the camaraderie that develops over the course of the class period.

Friendships between blacks and whites at the matric level are few: Nikki, a coloured girl, and Jill, a white girl, talk frequently during their prefect duty rounds. Ryan, an effeminate white boy who is ostracized from the whites at the school spends most of his time hanging onto a group of coloured girls. With good humor and some compassion, they tolerate his presence. Amanda, the head girl, who as previously noted, is of coloured and Indian background, moves easily among students of all races. Amanda, whose practices are an exception, will be discussed in the following chapter. But for the most part these relations are private—one-on-one friendships that exist within a limited sphere and immediately dissolve in the more open, public spaces of the field or the classroom.

For example, despite some of these friendships that cross racial lines, students at the matric dance (equivalent to a senior prom in the United States) seat themselves strictly by race—no one dares to move beyond the bounds and mores of their individual group, despite a potentially strong friendship with someone of another race. Even the group of African and coloured girls previously discussed do not cross the lines in this very public sphere. Instead, they sit separately, their friendships and connections confined to fleeting conversations in the relatively private space of the women's bathroom.

In the matric class at Fernwood, African and coloured students form an uneasy alliance, one that reflects the forces of the lingering politics of apartheid, specific class dynamics, and the racial politics of popular culture. As I will discuss in the following section, this alliance between African and coloured students is not maintained among the younger students at Fernwood.

CROSSROADS II: COLOUREDS, WHITES, AND RAVE

Four to five years younger than the matrics, grade 8 students at Fernwood face a different set of circumstances and a changed nexus of local and global racial conditions. Within Fernwood, as I have mentioned, the racial composition of the school shifts dramatically as one moves down from the senior class. In the younger grades African students vastly outnumber Indians, coloureds, and whites. Students in grade 8 no longer enter a school that is majority white; instead, Fernwood is majority African. Although coloured and African students in grade 12 may have created tenuous bonds to cope with their minority status in a white school, coloured and African students in grade 8 feel no such desire, or need. Hence the racial alliance, however thin, that manifests itself through the teasing practices and shared musical taste in grade 12 students is absent in grade 8.

A changing class composition is also an important component of the shifting racial alliances at Fernwood. While increasingly poor African students from the outlying townships stream into Fernwood, the younger coloured students are more likely to live in the formerly white area surrounding the school. This group of African and coloured students share little in common: Life experiences and language (many younger African students are only minimally proficient in English and coloured students rarely know even basic Zulu) separate them, and popular culture cannot be the solidifying bond that it is in grade 12.

In contrast, different configurations and patterns of alliance develop in grade 8. First, there is a small, though significant in its public prominence, amount of interracial dating, particularly between white boys and coloured girls. This type of interaction and connection is absent among older students, as Nikki, a coloured matric student, asserts, "She [speaking of a white girl] must go with a white guy. It's not right. Well, it's not not right. [4] They must go for their own kind. You would never get a coloured girl going with a white boy. It's just not the way it is." While from Nikki's position in the matric class dating between coloureds and whites is taboo, different dynamics dominate in grade 8.

One coloured girl, Sina, talks about this phenomenon, and notes the contradictions felt by her and her friends. When I ask her if she would ever date someone from a different racial group, she answers:

> Maybe white, but not black. I can't bring myself to, even talking to Gail [another coloured girl] she also said, she feels bad, we both feel bad because Shirley [a white girl] can bring herself to do it, and I can't and we are more black than her. I don't know, I can't. I just can't bring myself to kiss a black.

While older coloured girls at Fernwood might be just as likely to refuse to date an African boy, the level of discomfort and disgust expressed by Sina is more extreme and reflects the growing separation of African and coloured students in grade 8.

In addition to the shifts in dating patterns, musical tastes become blurred—many of the boundaries that are erected between coloureds and whites begin to break down. For example, among grade 12 students there are clear and sharp lines that divide "white" and "coloured" music, some of the politics of which were played out in the struggle over the fashion show. But in grade 8 the hardened lines around "white" and "coloured" music begin to soften. Popular culture thus plays a constitutive role in shaping and directing how racial and class bonds are envisioned and then enacted.

While over time there are undoubtedly numerous examples of this phenomenon, during the period of my research at Fernwood the most prominent case
involves the shift of "rave" music from an exclusively white practice to one that
encompasses both coloured and white students. In early 1996, most students identified rave music as a genre exclusively associated with whites. But then this preference begins to shift. Suddenly students are coming to school talking about "rave"
sessions at coloured clubs, and coloured students are beginning to find common
ground with white students because of and through the practice of raving. Not
insignificantly, this shift is most apparent among grade 8 students—the space in
the school in which links between coloureds and Africans are virtually nonexistent and the potential for connections between coloureds and white is the strongest.
Sina remarks on this growing phenomenon:

> The white and the coloured nation [5] are kind of mixed now, a lot of coloureds
> are going out with the whites, and even the dancing, in the clubs. Coloureds
> are even raving now, but at the beginning of the year it was only whites rav-
> ing. Now a lot of coloureds rave.

Later in our conversation, Sina notes that this alliance with white students breaks
the historic ties between coloureds and Africans:

> Coloureds and blacks [Africans] have a similar way of thinking but coloureds
> get along better with whites . . . . I think what mainly brought the coloureds
> and whites together was rave dancing . . . . If there are two races that get along
> well it's coloureds and Indians. Now Indians have also started mixing with
> white. It's those three races that get along quite well.

Note the contrast between Sina's reading of the social relations of her grade 8
world, with that of Rosa, a white matric student, who comments on her attempts
to get her coloured friends to listen to rave:

> I was talking the other day, I was telling Melissa and Nikki that they must
> come to the Med [a white club in town] because they don't listen to rave music
> or anything, so Melissa said, what is that. She didn't even know. But they
> normally listen to r and b, things like that. The music is different.

Divisions that are accepted as normal and everyday at the matric level are no
longer as strong or evident among grade 8 students. Although Nikki and Melissa,
two coloured matric girls, would never consider going to a rave or listening to rave
music (and apparently don't even know what it is), Sina, in grade 8, embraces rave
and by extension alliances with white students.

Students such as Sina understand fully that there is a shift in racial alliances
at Fernwood, and attribute the break in the coloured-African connection to
changing affiliations in the world of popular culture. Marlene, an Indian student
who spends time with coloured students comments on this phenomenon: "I did-
n't used to like rave music, but now I like it." Marlene also notes that her taste in

clothing is shifting. "That's more r and b [the checked shirts], sometimes we, I still have my old clothes, I like them. But you rather dress up in those shiny things because you are at a rave." Marlene's ambivalence towards her "old clothes" reveals not simply a change in taste, but a subtle shift in the ways in which she thinks about and lives out a racialized identity. As she moves from a preference for r and b (a shared taste with black students) to rave, she as an Indian student takes up a new position within the school (and, notably, a position somewhat different from her older sister, a grade 11 student). The movement of rave from whites to whites and coloureds (and Indians) happens rapidly—coloured clubs add special rave sessions, and when I spend a week at a coloured school during this period the students generally confirm that coloured taste is shifting towards raving.

Coloureds' and whites' shared practice of raving, based partially in the dynamics of class, signals a shift in the racial alliances at Fernwood with potential future consequences for the racial politics of the school. As Paul Gilroy (1987) writes in the case of Britain, "A political relationship between Afro-Caribbeans and Asians on which the future of black Britain may depend is being created in these cultural encounters" (p. 218). Although the implications of the bonds at Fernwood are quite different, the future dynamics of the school may depend on the burgeoning cultural encounters between coloureds and whites, which break older cultural alliances between coloureds and Africans. In the case of youth at Fernwood, the stream of global cultural flows runs through and remaps these relations.

THE NUANCES OF CHANGING BORDERS

Fernwood students most obviously are not the first South Africans to encounter the borders between racialized groups. Inevitably and by design, Africans, Indians, coloured, and whites moved in contiguous and overlapping spaces. Yet these apartheid borders were saturated with inequality. For example, Africans lived in white households, cared for their children, cooked their meals, and washed their clothes. However, legal and economic barriers defined the limits and possibilities of these relationships (though, of course, there were exceptions and breaks). Fernwood students, in contrast, must engage with borders that are in persistent flux. Old ones have collapsed, yet the new is not fully formed. The racialized borders between students are reinvigorated through the politics of taste, as students mark and guard the boundaries between themselves and "the other." White students, angry and frustrated with societal changes, try to prop up the old borders—to reassert their superiority in a school in which they are quickly losing their footing.

In the midst of the ongoing conflict, there are flashes of connection that point to other, emerging dynamics. African and coloured students in grade 12 find solidarity in the shared experiences of being a minority in a predominantly white school, in their similar class background, and in their shared taste preferences. These factors allow these African and coloured grade 12 students to draw a line, a border, between themselves and white students. But at the other end of the school, students only four to five years younger envision their racialized borders differently—here, white students align themselves with coloureds (and the few Indian students), and Africans are forced to the other side of the divide. Taste plays its role here too, as rave music becomes the practice that joins coloured, white, and Indians in a new alliance.

The changing nuances of the borders at Fernwood do not simply arise in a mechanistic or predetermined manner from reforming societal dynamics. Groups of students test out and play with the spaces in-between: They open them up to explore the possibilities that now exist, possibilities that were severely curtailed and closed off previously. These changes reverberate not only within the small circles of these students' friendships, but throughout the school, as others watch the emerging patterns and follow them. In this chapter I have charted group dynamics that rework racialized border spaces; in the following chapter I highlight the practices of seven individual students and the ways that their responses to the social world of Fernwood shape the future of race.

CHAPTER SEVEN

THE TEXTURE OF THE BORDER:
PORTRAITS OF INDIVIDUAL STUDENTS

In the two previous chapters, I have focused attention on the generalized racial dynamics at Fernwood and the ways in which the politics of taste become a constituent element of their unfolding. In this final ethnographic chapter, I move from broad, thematic sweeps to intimate portraits of individual students. In relating their experiences of Fernwood, I examine how these seven individuals make sense of their lives in one of the spaces of newness, a multiracial school, that has emerged in South Africa in the 1990s. The politics of taste, as played out through an engagement with the popular, are ever-present, but are here contextualized within local dynamics that include Fernwood, Durban, and South Africa.

The students discussed here are not necessarily representative of Fernwood students, nor is my analysis exhaustive of the possible positions that are available to students. Both my theoretical interests and personal experiences of Fernwood (see appendix) drew me to the border spaces of the school, where race is actively confronted and negotiated. As a result, there are students to whom I had little or no access (most notably, more assertively racist white students), and there are quite clearly stories that are excluded. Additionally, given my relatively greater access to girls (discussed in the appendix), they figure prominently in these stories, accounting for six of the seven students discussed. But I have selected these stories not for their statistical representativeness, but because they are compelling in and of themselves: each student profiled in some way reinscribing, reconfiguring, or challenging the racial borders that exist at Fernwood. I write and read these stories as tales of possibility, or what Homi Bhabha ("The third space," 1990) refers to as a "third space," which cracks open the myth of fixed selves and allows for a reimagining of the contours of the politics of race.

Coloured students at Fernwood often see themselves as "in-between": constantly negotiating the space between themselves and whites and themselves and Africans. They fit cleanly within neither the African nor white side of the racial divide, simultaneously constituting their own group marked by taste, and flirting close to the lines that define both white and African. Additionally, because of historical and often familial ties between coloureds and Indians, there are also complex dynamics in their relations that are characterized both by disdain and dislike, and connection and friendship.

The three coloured students I discuss respond in different ways to occupying the space in-between. The first student, Nikki, attempts to create a solid identity for herself as a coloured, but allows for alliances with African students. The second student, Charmaine, identifies the way that music has shifted her coloured identity—while she still sees herself as coloured, it is a more expansive, less essentialized view of that racial position than Nikki holds. The third student, Amanda, finds herself simultaneously positioned as white and black, as she struggles to move between the segregated world of her neighborhood and the multiracial world of Fernwood.

White students, in contrast, approach the racial borders at Fernwood from a different angle. Not positioned in-between, they imagine and construct a firmer line between themselves and black students, which they reconfigure and cross in different ways. The first student, Jackie, is one of the few white students at school who shows an affinity for African musical taste, particularly rap music. Although Jackie meets up with black students in the realm of global popular culture, local racial politics keep them separate within the bounds of South Africa and Fernwood. The second white student, Shirley, is one of the few students at Fernwood to deliberately flaunt racial borders—taking her white body and placing it within territory that is firmly marked as coloured.

The two African students I profile, Zola and Molefe, take different positions vis-à-vis the borderlands: Zola is angry about the institutional structures of the school that she views as racist, but she is unconcerned about, and often indifferent to, her white, coloured, and Indian classmates. In contrast, Molefe struggles to make friends and smooth over the tensions of the past, seeing himself as a representative of the African community. But this representation is never complete nor total, as Molefe stands outside of, and critiques, this same community.

Not all these border crossings are positive moments: These are not necessarily happy minglings of races and cultures. Instead, these students' experiences exemplify the tensions and contradictions of negotiating race in a conflict-ridden atmosphere. Here, I mean to explore the hybridity (Bhabha's third space), that opens up within many of the students' practices of identity. As Bhabha comments, ". . . the importance of hybridity is not to be able to trace two original moments from which the third emerges, rather hybridity to me is the 'third space' which enables other positions to emerge" (1990, p. 211). The portraits of many of the students in this section demonstrate the multiplicity of "third spaces," or forms of hybridity, that are possible and arise within the confines of Fernwood. These configurations are inherently new, as they are formed within a space—that of a multiracial school—that has few precedents in South Africa. As Bhabha argues, "The process of cultural hybridity gives rise to something different, something new and unrecognisable, a new area of negotiation of meaning and representation" (p. 211). The hybrid that emerges here does not look backward to construct and reconstruct her origins, but forward to the possibilities that her existence enables.

NIKKI: BEING COLOURED

Nikki, more than perhaps any other coloured student at Fernwood, crafts a coloured identity for herself that incorporates the practices of taste, but is also grounded in strong political views. I use "political" here not to signal Nikki's allegiance to any particular political party in South Africa—she knows little about that and has no affiliation—but to mark that Nikki has thought about the position of coloureds in both apartheid and post-apartheid society and can articulate specific ideas about her solution to the tensions of a multiracial society.

Nikki scrupulously follows coloured taste preferences in music and clothing, rejecting, for example, shoes that she labels as "white." Being coloured is a crucial part of her identity and, as a matric student, she feels a compelling duty to model appropriate taste choices for younger coloured youth. Her allegiance to the taste codes of coloureds comes at some cost and sacrifice for her mother, Nikki's sole financial support. The family, which includes Nikki, her mother, and two other grown children who live at home intermittently to save money, reside in a small, cramped house in a working-class coloured area.

The "colouredness" that Nikki embraces and advocates has three imperatives: (1) that coloureds unite; (2) recognize, create, and sustain connections with Africans; and (3) reject any connections with whites. She comments:

> Coloured people are delayed. How many coloureds have you ever seen on TV, and all this, standing up for coloured rights. There's no one that I know. You get the odd few that go out and have a couple things to say, but they are either standing for what the blacks believe in, or what the whites believe in, but nobody stands up for the coloured people.

Thus, Nikki asserts frustration with the lack of a clear, well-articulated coloured perspective within South African politics, and yearns for this unity of purpose. Nikki's solution to South Africa's problems is one that many would view as rather drastic:

> I know it's a racist point of view, but I believe, I believe in apartheid, but not in the sense of depriving people of anything. I believe coloureds with coloureds,

whites with whites, blacks with blacks, Indians with Indians. I believe that the Indians should be in India, I know that's mean, but I believe the coloureds should be in the Cape, the whites should be back in Europe, and the blacks should have the rest of South Africa, it belongs to them. Give everyone equal rights, give everybody the chance to make their own rules, but just take them out of each other's way. Because that's what causes conflict.

Despite her preference for separation, Nikki forges tight personal ties with African girls at school and feels that there is a natural affinity between Africans and coloureds, based primarily on shared taste in music and fashion and a similar sense of fun. Nikki comments that even though she feels that coloureds are penalized by affirmative action policies, she does not blame Africans. "Personally I have nothing against blacks, I like them, I really do. Because we have fun with them." This preference also extends to whom she feels comfortable welcoming to her home. As a participant in a student exchange program within South Africa, Nikki is often asked to host other students visiting from various parts of the country. She relates that she refused to host a white girl:

Even when I had the girls from Cape Town, they wanted to give me a white girl. I said I don't want a white girl, I don't want an Indian girl, I'd rather have a black or a coloured. They are culturally inclined. I can get along with the black kids better than I can with a white.

Nikki vehemently rejects any connection between coloureds and whites, commenting here on the different ways that whites and coloureds eat:

Like eating with a knife and fork, you mainly find that in white families. I mean, when I went to my cousin's house I couldn't [note: her cousin married a white man]. I eat with just my fork only and I really don't eat with a knife and fork, and they don't call it supper, they call it dinner . . . . I mean I couldn't live like that.

Nikki also relates that, in her opinion, whites and coloureds could never live together harmoniously, as coloureds and Africans could. When I ask her why a white would never move into a coloured area, she replies:

Because they feel it's unsafe, because they don't like the way they live, black people's culture, they must make noise and shout and scream, and white people don't do that. I mean, I went to stay in that situation with my cousin . . . . and I couldn't. Playing the radio, just for ourselves in the house, really, really soft. You stand outside you can hear a pin drop, it's dead quiet. Now when I'm home in our area, kids are playing in the road, screaming and shouting. Kids are on the road, radios are on loud, and it's so different than the white areas.

Nikki constructs her coloured identity in affiliation with Africans, noting parallels in both taste preferences and lifestyles. Whites and Indians are rejected as incompatible with the crucial elements of a coloured lifestyle—this despite her admission that her heritage is part white and Indian, her best friend is half Indian, and many of her friends, including me, are white. Nikki struggles to retain what she sees and believes is essential to coloured separateness, quashing her attraction to a white boy at school because "you would never get a coloured girl going with white boys. It's just not the way it is."

Nikki illustrates the parameters of one variation of coloured identity at Fern-wood. As one of the original group of coloured and African students who integrated Fernwood, Nikki's affinities lie with Africans, who also suffered alienation and iso-lation in a then majority white school. To maintain her colouredness, she rejects ties with whites—ties that the younger students at Fernwood both create and cele-brate. Despite her steadfast embrace of colouredness, she has more white friends that most coloured matric students at Fernwood, and moves easily between segregated groups of Indians, Africans, whites, and coloureds. Nikki's response to negotiating a new reality is to move toward a solid racial identity—an attempt to recreate bor-ders and boundaries in a situation that could just as easily lead to their disintegra-tion. She is not, however, wholly successful at maintaining these parameters. Although she consciously tries to push back anything that may hint at hybridity, or a shift in a "pure" coloured identity, it proves to be impossible. She is unable to go back, to recreate an authentic coloured identity for herself grounded in her coloured township and isolated experience. The "originary" eludes her—she must recreate colouredness on new terrain as she can no longer claim to live a coloured existence that is wholly separate from connections with Africans, Indians, and whites.

Nikki's story contrasts with that of the two other coloured students I will discuss, Charmaine and Amanda, both of whom push at the very borders Nikki tries to hold on to and police.

CHARMAINE: REJECTING AND REINVENTING RACE

Charmaine, a grade 11 student at Fernwood, resists the idea of racial classifica-tion, wishing that such identifications would disappear in the new South Africa. She writes:

> As a result of my father being Indian and my mother coloured it is difficult for people to distinguish my race. I am often asked about my race and this aggra-vates me as I believe that in the New South Africa race is over-emphasized.

Charmaine finds race to be a limiting category, one that she wants to escape. Yet, at the same time, she notes that her own sense of identity is grounded in those very practices. Charmaine attended a more prestigious, predominantly white girls school before transferring to Fernwood, and notes this impact on her identity:

> It's changed so much for me. I went to a mixed school. I listen to what is termed white music. I like techno and stuff like that. It's because I go to a white school, and I mix with white people, so it does change your identity.

In this observation, Charmaine never argues that she has become white, but that her identity has been transformed through a change in taste. Her preference for what she refers to as white music (i.e., techno,) indicates that she is no longer solidly located as a coloured, which she defines through taste preferences. Because of these differences, she can never totally identify with other (grade 11 and 12) coloured students at Fernwood—racial solidarity is fractured through a shift in musical taste.

Yet neither is Charmaine white; even if she desired to enter into that affiliation through changing her taste, the racial polarization of the school and society prohibits it. Commenting on her feeling towards her white friends, Charmaine says, "I know that even though I have white friends, they still look down on me in a way now, deep down inside. They wouldn't say it but sometimes you overhear them talking." Charmaine occupies a third space, one that embodies the tensions of trying to cross borders.

But the borders themselves are never solid. For example, when I interviewed Charmaine early in the year, she identified particular music, (i.e., techno) as white music. And thus her affinity for techno music caused her to resituate her identity, moving herself out of the solid category of coloured, but not fully into the category of white. Yet, as the borders of what defines "white" and "coloured" music are reconfigured through the year, the poles of racial identity can shift also. Younger coloured students at Fernwood may not see techno music as an exclusively white practice, thus an affinity for such music may not signal, for them, a shift in identity. They are no longer crossing a troublesome and rocky border in order to enjoy techno music—instead, they have the option of continuing to see themselves as solidly coloured yet connected with white students in an affective alliance. But for Charmaine, a grade 11 student, her passion for techno music separates her from what she understands as a coloured identity, pushing her away from students such as Nikki, and towards an awkward and uncertain encounter with whiteness.

AMANDA: OCCUPYING MULTIPLE RACIAL POSITIONS

Having spent her whole life attending white schools, Amanda skirts the edges of whiteness—knowing intimately its contours, mannerisms, dress, and tastes, but yet clearly also knowing that she is not. Of coloured and Indian background, Amanda grew up in an Indian area, a decision that her parents made, according to Amanda, to protect her from negative behavioral influences in coloured areas. As Amanda relates, "My mom felt that a coloured area would be too wild, and she feels that I needed to be in an environment that was stable and wasn't wild, and to be in a quiet environment." The decision to send her to white schools was a difficult one for her father, who, as Amanda frames it, was a "victim of apartheid." As a result, she says, "He's not racist or anything, it's just that, towards white people, he doesn't often take a liking to them immediately, he feels that he can't trust them." Despite her father's feelings, Amanda attended a multiracial convent school until grade 8, and then entered Fernwood. The priorities of a "good education and a good, solid grounding" for his daughter and his concerns about her future were more important than his personal fears and mistrust.

Within the bounds of Fernwood, Amanda feels that she must continually try to prove that she is worthy of attending a white school and having white friends. She recalls:

> When I first came to Fernwood, because apartheid was just like, in its final stages, and I often had to justify who I was, the color of my skin. And even now today, the government's been in practice for two years; they claim that apartheid is done away with, but even today I feel that I always have to justify to people who I am.

Amanda feels strongly that it is necessary "to forgive, but don't forget. Don't forget what happened to you, but it's in the past, just leave it." She is frustrated by the reluctance of other students to mix, and positions herself and her own identity as flexible—one that can change and transform itself as necessary. She says, "I'm just a person who can mix. I can fit into any group, and I'm not scared to make the change." At one point, she comments that most of her friends are white, but then later begins to enumerate her friendships with coloureds, Indians, and Africans. She knows that her connections with students of all races lead to comments and labeling. "If I am with one specific race group, then I'm often labeled. Like you know Molefe, Joseph, and Thandeka, those are my friends. One of the whites remarked that I just love all the black people."

Yet Amanda, like many black students at Fernwood, has had to tolerate both the taunting of her black peers who do not attend white schools and the continuing racism of white students, teachers, and administrators at Fernwood. She relates:

> Often, when I walk on the road in my area, because they all know I go to a white school, one guy turned around and said to me, look how high she holds her nose up in the air. She's actually blocking the sun. She thinks she's white.

When I ask Amanda what is meant by "She thinks she's white," she replies, "To them, white ways are, like I listen to some of the white music . . . . I dress in a certain way and do things in a certain way. I don't talk slang, and I don't act the way they act." As Amanda states, "whiteness" becomes associated with particular types of music and dress—taste again being used to define racial borders. Other practices, particularly that of language and personal style, are also invoked.

While Amanda's musical taste may cross over into white territory, her taste in clothing remains coloured—she does not adopt the casual, thrown together style of white students. In contrast, Amanda is extremely conscious of her clothing choices—wearing only what is the latest coloured fashion, extremely neat, tailored, and often elegant. If Amanda is influenced by any racially based taste codes in addition to those of coloured students, it is Africans, not whites, who provide her with a role model. But her emphasis on style is interpreted by adolescents in her neighborhood as trying to "look white," while within the confines of Fernwood that same emphasis separates her, undeniably, from whites. Thus, the same clothes that function to mark "white" in one particular site (the Indian area where she lives) simultaneously mark her as "black" in another (Fernwood). Amanda's "racial" self shifts as she moves from one geographic locale to another.

Perhaps because Amanda is simultaneously coded as "white" and "black" she can cross and transgress borders with ease—moving in African, coloured, Indian, and white social circles at Fernwood. She pushes at the borders of what it means to be coloured at Fernwood—retaining, in general, the markers of coloured identity through clothing, but reworking the other borders of coloured. Amanda refuses to let taste categories dictate her identity. Instead, she plays with these limits by listening to white music while simultaneously having African friends. By moving between segregated spheres and occupying several racial positions at once, Amanda confounds the racial commonsense that governs the social space at Fernwood. She jumps borders with ease and, in the process, opens up a new site of identity for herself.

JACKIE: HOSTILITY AT THE BORDER

For Jackie, a white grade 11 student, the end of apartheid has meant uncertainty and confusion. Jackie's confusion is expressed in her contradictory belief that change has both been substantial and nonexistent. For example, while she is still visibly shocked when she sees Africans who are wealthier than she is, Jackie is also perplexed to see many Africans whose material existence has altered little since the end of apartheid. She says:

> but what is the weirdest thing is that even though everybody has equal rights, I still see the same people on the street, the people from before apartheid. We used to live in town, near the Playhouse, and we had this old black man come and sing in our road, and people would throw coins at him . . . . And I went to visit a friend of mine, and I happened to be staying late into the night, and the man still came there, he sang there. He was like half blind and he was still doing it, even though we supposedly have equal rights.

Unable to understand that political rights do not automatically translate into economic equality, Jackie is dejected and pessimistic about the future possibilities for South Africa, a position she shares with many of her white classmates at Fernwood.

For Jackie and a small group of white students, part of the answer to their ongoing confusion and anxiety is found in gangsta rap: music normally not associated with whites at Fernwood. Their preference for gangsta rap separates them from other whites; Jackie and her friends sit in a small, isolated group every break, cut off from other white students because of differences in musical taste. Jackie rejects the techno music preferred by other whites, and explains her attraction to gangsta rap:

> It's so true to life, a lot of gangsta rap they do tend to go on about black peo-
> ple and how they have their problems and stuff, but in other ways it's cool to
> listen to, their points of view about what happens in South Central and stuff.

Jackie responds differently than other white students to the violence she sees around her by trying to understand and contextualize her experiences. Like some of the African students she sees her reality reflected in gangsta rap:

> It's like thinking about what could probably happen in South Africa in a cou-
> ple of years, we will probably have gangs like that doing stuff, because it seems
> almost inevitable that is what is going to come to South Africa.

Instead of trying to escape the violence like other whites, Jackie embraces it—she gets "pumped up." She feels that, like Africans, she is living in the "hood," and the music of the hood is her music too.

But an affinity for gangsta rap is the only thing that Jackie shares with African students at Fernwood. The connections that they make in the public sphere of global popular culture do not translate into any sort of alliance at school or outside of it. [1] The clubs that Jackie frequents play gangsta rap for virtually all white audiences. The music serves not as a way of building bridges between whites and Africans, but as a vehicle for whites to express their resentment and hostility towards Africans and the destruction and violence that whites perceive they have brought to South Africa. Not being able to historicize and contextualize the specifics of violence, Jackie equates the historical "war-like" behavior of Zulus with the contemporary violence of South Africa and the ghettos of Los Angeles—African violence is uni-versalized. Jackie's relationship to gangsta rap shares both points of congruency and divergence with that of white adolescents in the United States who constitute gangsta rap's biggest audience. Part of its attraction is in its evocation of black authenticity and a primitive violence that, as previously discussed, Jackie associates with Africans worldwide. But unlike white adolescents in the United States, Jackie does not listen to gangsta rap to be a voyeur of the black experience, as scholars such as Ewan Allinson (1994) argue. Her interaction with blacks is immediate and per-sonal; she does not need to travel, either with her body or her mind, to experience the other. Instead, she uses gangsta rap as a way of *explaining* the dynamics of the sit-uation in which she finds herself: surrounded by blacks.

In rejecting the norms of whiteness that prevail at Fernwood, Jackie does create a new space of identity. The happy, childlike, feel-good escapism of raves is foreign to her. Her whiteness confronts the border with African students in a contradictory way—she embraces their music, but as a way of releasing her hos-tility and anger. A border is crossed, but this is not a happy mixing—instead it a violent, rage filled confrontation with difference.

SHIRLEY: TRANSGRESSING BORDERS

At the center of the controversy about race, racial identity, and border crossing at Fernwood sits Shirley. Fourteen years old, blonde, and freckled, Shirley typifies in many ways the average white student at Fernwood. From a conservative, Afrikaner background, Shirley used to live with her grandmother, but is now back, at least temporarily, with her mother. Her father is not in the immediate area and she sees him only on holidays. Shirley struggles with academics, often looks disheveled, and is not afraid of a fight. She is, these days, the sort of white student whom Fernwood both needs and detests.

But unlike virtually every other white student at Fernwood, Shirley refuses to respect the spoken and unspoken borders between races. Her closest friends at Fernwood are a group of coloured girls and her transgressions are the talk of both students and staff. As Shirley explains:

> Last year we used to have a lot of fights. All because I was with different races. So girls used to pick on me. Once there was a big fight. I almost hit the prefect. The girls said that coloureds are sluts and bitches, and the white people rule and everything. I've got a reputation in school, and if someone tells me something, and I know it's not right, I'm going to go and tell them and I will fight them.

What, in the eyes of Fernwood students and staff, makes Shirley coloured? For some, it's her speech patterns—she "talks like a coloured." Her speech seems to particularly irritate teachers, including Donna Westoff, who, while discussing Shirley in the staff room one day, threatened to "wash her mouth out with soap"— a comment that other staff either agreed with or ignored. Shirley is aware of Ms. Westoff's feelings, and relates this story:

> Some of the teachers really pick on me. There's one teacher, Ms. Westoff. I was walking down the stairs with two friends, and I was teasing them, and Ms. Westoff says "Change your ways." Who has the right to tell me to change my ways? What's it got to do with her? It's not her daughter that's holding a black child.

Shirley's friend, Helen, accuses another teacher of trying to separate Shirley from her coloured friends, "Even Ms. Munz, she saw Shirley hanging around with us and all of that. And every break she used to take Shirley away from us and make her pick up litter."

Despite the uproar and disapproval that Shirley's friendships cause among teachers and many of the older students at Fernwood, the younger students are split. Some mimic the reactions of their older peers, including Rob, a white boy, who asked, "It makes me mad, why doesn't she want to go with her own nation, why does she have to act coloured?" But others are accepting of her behavior, and see her as part of an emerging trend in which whites "act coloured" by adopting coloured taste in fashion and music. Sina, a coloured student, remarks on this trend: "I've noticed there are a lot of white pupils, in Fernwood especially, who want to be coloured. I think you know." When I ask Sina what she meant by they want to be coloured, she replies, "The dress, you know, most of the coloureds have a style of dressing, the Dickies. Most of them are changing to that way. Talk like this, express themselves in that way." Rena, a coloured, student comments specifically on Shirley. "She doesn't know how whites dress, she dresses like us. She listens to our music, follows our music. Our jeans, not theirs." Sina combines two discursive constructions of race, one that situates race as culture, in this case, speech, and the other that constructs race as a matter of taste. Rena marks racial lines clearly through taste and indicates that Shirley's taste leaves her with an identity, an affiliation, that is, ambivalently, coloured.

From the students' perspective, Shirley's behavior cannot be described as imitating coloured students—the seriousness of her transgression lies in her flaunting of accepted racialized taste divisions. By crossing these lines, Shirley is expressing more than a wish or a fantasy—she is adopting tangible, material aspects of coloured identity. In doing so, she confounds the racial commonsense that exists at Fernwood, which tries to lock students into solid racial identities through regulating their clothing and musical tastes. Shirley's behavior exposes the constructed nature of these categories. While the teachers read her racial identity through her associations with coloured girls and her speech patterns, students hone in on those aspects of racial identity that are most critical for them: her taste in fashion and music. When Shirley herself describes her behavior, she invokes taste categories to signal her border crossing:

> If I go out with a boy who's white, we don't like each other's music, we don't like how each other dresses. He goes to here, I go to places here. He don't like the places we go to. With a coloured boy, I know what he likes, he knows what I like.

By boldly and deliberately stepping outside of prescribed lines, Shirley becomes a target for teachers and students who disapprove of her actions.

Shirley is not the sole border transgressor at Fernwood. Other students, for example, Ryan, have friends who are of different races. But Shirley is unusual in several ways. First, she is not a well-behaved, docile student, but attracts attention because of her propensity for fighting and her outspoken nature. Second, Shirley is one of the few students who actively adopts the taste codes of other racial groups. Although some students have friendships that cross racial divides, it is rarer for a student to openly and publicly flaunt the music and clothes that defines their racial group. Most students wait for a large group of their peers to shift taste (as in the example of rave) before crossing themselves. In daring to play with race, Shirley becomes the fulcrum for sustained scrutiny and fury at Fernwood.

ZOLA: INDIFFERENCE AT THE BORDER

For African students like Zola, the borders are a minefield. She must contend with the institutional structures and realities of a white school, while negotiating the racial dynamics of her peers both at Fernwood and at home in the township of

Umlazi. Despite these pressures, Zola accepts that her reality simply is what it is; she feels little inclination to try to improve her situation, and is generally content.

Zola came to Fernwood at her parents' suggestion, but was not opposed to it. She remembers, "I was kind of keen, how it was like to be in a white school." Similar to a number of her African peers in the matric class, she attended an (African) convent school (usually with white teachers) during her primary school years and was thus prepared, both psychologically and academically, to attend a formerly white high school. Zola's feelings about Fernwood are mixed; while she is happy to be receiving an education that will prepare her to attend a technikon, she resents the administration's attitude towards students. She still feels bitter about an incident that happened several years ago, when she was a member of the school choir:

> The first two years, I was a soloist, we used to sing for the school. And we never got any rewards. I mean, that's bad. We used to come on Saturdays and Sundays, maybe the whole cast would come on Saturdays and the two soloists had to come on Sunday as well. Imagine coming Saturday, Sunday, and during the week . . . . We didn't even get a merit certificate. Some people who were in the cast, they got scrolls. We didn't even get a cent, the soloists. We paid our money for transport to come to school. So I said never do anything for Fernwood. I'll never do any sports.

Yet Zola, like every other Fernwood student, is required to stay after school several times a week during the athletics (track and field) season to practice to represent Fernwood. She hates it, and her animosity towards the school festers.

But her negative feelings towards the white administrators do not extend to her peers. Despite her recognition of the racism of many of her white classmates, she seems to have few strong feelings against them, seeing it as a rather minor area of disagreement:

> Some people are racialistic. When you learn about South African history, then they tell you blacks are inferior, whites are superior. And now you think about it, it's really bad for you, you have to say, no, no, no, it doesn't go that way. Because you were not given a chance. Then you go through a lot of discussions. But anyway it's fine, it depends who you are talking to and who you stay with. If you act like you don't like blacks, then I act like I don't like whites. If you like me, I like you back. If you don't like me, then I just don't like you.

Many of the divides with white students are seen as naturalized and grounded both in language differences and in taste:

> I can mix with whites, but, I can tell a nice story in Zulu, we have fun, but when you change it into English it's not as nice. They're not going to enjoy it as with the black kids. You can say something in Zulu and it can be nice, and you change it into English and it can be boring. And anyway, we don't like the same things, we don't go to the same places. She's going to tell me

about the nightclub she went to, I'm not interested in her nightclub. I say oh yeah, fine. I'm not interested.

Zola, like other students, also rattles off a long list of differences based on clothes and music. Yet here, boredom and indifference, as opposed to hostility, structure Zola's encounters with white students at Fernwood. White students, for Zola, exist as a constant, now common and accepted, facet of daily life. She feels little need or desire to communicate with them. Although Zola has a few white friends at school, the relationships are limited due to larger societal dynamics:

> you can have a white friend at school, do everything with her, but you can't go to her place, you think what are her friends going to say, she's bringing black people around.

Similarly, Zola comments that it would be impossible for her to bring a white friend to the township where she lives:

> Let's say in the township I'll have a friend from Fernwood come to visit me, they'll say you think you're white and everything. Those who are jealous . . . . People are jealous. Some people are jealous that you are in the white school. They say it's the same education, but you know it's not the same education. Maybe next year, maybe in the future it's going to start to be the same education, but now it's not the same education.

For Zola, there are few incentives to befriend white students. She realizes many harbor racist feelings, and while she is open to friendly communication and interchange with anyone, including whites, there appears to be little to be gained from close friendships with whites. In any case, these relationships would, of necessity, be limited to the space of the school as blacks and whites share few common interests and cannot comfortably visit each other at home. Zola's story is typical of many African matric students at Fernwood. They feel discomfort with, though not hostility towards, their white classmates. They are pleased to be in a white school, and grateful for the opportunities that will be available to them in the future, yet they are still aware of the institutional structures that deny them opportunity and recognition. Race continues to hold meaning, though more at the level of institutional and societal structures than in personal relationships. Difference is defined through multiple coordinates: where one lives, and the ever-present music and clothing. Yet difference is not a major concern for Zola; she walks multiple borders daily, yet with a certain ease and some resignation to the reality of the world she inhabits now and will face in the future.

MOLEFE: WALKING A SLIPPERY BORDER

From a politically involved and visible family, Molefe feels a strong responsibility to excel at Fernwood and to serve as a positive representative of the African community. He relates:

now I'm in a white school, so I represent the community that I come from, so I have to set a very good example to the other races. Because I know some people are misinformed about the township, I feel like it's my duty to set things straight, to know what the township is like, because every time they see on TV they see violence, so they think all the townships are the same.

Molefe's quest to influence the attitudes and opinions of (primarily) whites towards Africans may reflect his lingering feelings of inferiority. He remembers that his family instilled in him the belief that he would need to fight to be seen and accepted as equal to whites, that equality would not be a given in South African society. He recalls that

I always believed that, I'm black okay, so I believed that the person who is not black, I believe I'm inferior to that person, especially to the whites . . . . The whites are superior. But when I came to this school, I learned to adjust from being inferior to being equal, that's a very big adjustment from being inferior to being equal.

Despite Molefe's efforts to overcome these feelings, they persist and, as he comments, affect his relationships with white students at Fernwood:

I don't think it's a problem for me to get used to a different race. The only problem is the first time: if it's a white person and you are a black person you have to draw back a little bit. It just happens. I don't know what causes it. You just drop back a little bit.

Molefe is keen to influence attitudes and behaviors, to make friends, and to smooth over relations from the past. The border is still a hierarchical boundary, and he believes that the best way to change the systems that structure black lives is to win the "hearts and minds" of the whites who now surround him. Race, and the problems of racism, is deeply embedded in his personal relationships. While Zola situates "race" as a complication of institutional structures, "race" for Molefe is located in the personal and in the everyday.

It is evident that Molefe does not identify with the white students who surround him, nor with the white administrators or teachers. While he accepts that their world is the one in which he must prove his ability and intelligence, he does not "act white" (Fordham, 1988;1996), nor does he attempt to assimilate, or take on, wholesale, an "identity." He strives not to be them, but to be accepted as equal, in an environment in which he is fully aware that he is not, despite the political end of apartheid.

At the same time, Molefe is critical of and somewhat distant from the African community (as he defines it). Here he comments on what he perceives as laziness within the community: "...some of the blacks they don't like to go and learn. They don't like to go to school, they want to sit down and have things handed out, they don't want to work for everything." Later, he observes that this lack of commitment and drive extends to those who are in positions of power and influence, "[There are] some people in government who earn fat checks, who drive luxury cars, who stay in nice houses, and they don't do anything for the community." Thus, Molefe expresses his frustrations with the community from which he came—it can provide no more of a "home," no more of a space for identification and belonging than the white-dominated world of Fernwood. Molefe must negotiate between two worlds, but neither is comfortable. While he inhabits a border space in the new opening made possible by the end of legal apartheid, Molefe does not combine and mix aspects of the two sides of the borders, but rejects both. At Fernwood, he feels compelled to "represent" a community from which he is, in large measure, estranged. The border here is full of tension and provides not sure footing or even a temporary resting place, but a ledge so slick that moving forward, catapulting oneself towards the new and unexplored, is the only option.

Molefe's feelings about the future, both for himself and South Africa, are mixed. On the one hand, he is deeply pessimistic about what he sees as the escalating violence and predicts, "I see the country going down to poverty because no one's going to school. In KwaMashu [an African township] people are killing the teachers. If you kill the only person who can save you, definitely you are going nowhere. I don't see the rest of the country going anywhere." Despite this expressed despair, he still believes in the potential for the African community to change and believes that he has a role in its transformation. He relates:

> In the township, we've got very few models you can look up to . . . . I can be a role model for kids, and they see me, and they can say we grew up with him and he turned out to be something good. So they can also do something good and they can go to school, and improve on their academics. That's the only way I know for blacks in this country to flourish if they go to school and study.

Molefe may find himself inhabiting an uncomfortable border, but for him there is little other choice; neither side of the divide can provide an anchor. As he writes, "This nation has proven to be a mixture of different challenges and I have to get through all this [sic] challenges by myself." So he moves forward, retaining the hope that as he proceeds he can encourage and cajole others in the African community to follow him and simultaneously convince whites, Indians, and coloureds that their fears are misplaced. As Molefe insists:

> I believe that the place is big enough for all of us. Our hearts are big enough to love everyone. The whites, and the coloureds and the Indians they mustn't be scared, because there's nothing to be scared for . . . . If everyone looked deep down in their hearts, they'd know that our hearts are big enough to love everyone.

REFLECTING ON THE BORDER

Conceptually, borders are a key feature of the spatial map of Fernwood. The political and legal collapse of the imposed borders of apartheid has, of course, not led

to their equally swift demise in the daily lives of South Africans, including Fernwood students. Instead, the contours and textures of the borders are open for
change and reconfiguration: the possibilities of what one does with the borders,
how they are approached, what they mean, and what they enable and close down,
expand. As I have demonstrated, this does not mean that all potential reworkings
of the border are necessarily liberatory or positive. Nikki resists change at the same
time that she is hopelessly immersed within it; Jackie's encounters with African
students at Fernwood allow her "authentic" contact with the violent lives portrayed in rap music. In other instances, the opening of borders creates painful and
uncomfortable spaces: Molefe's anguish is palpable, as he is repeatedly rejected by
the white world and simultaneously distant from the black one. Amanda, in contrast, boldly embraces the new world she inhabits. Less concerned with other people's perspectives, Amanda is not trapped by the border. Instead, she simultaneously negotiates multiple racial positions, trailblazing possibilities for negotiating
identity. In a different, perhaps more constrained manner, Charmaine also rein-
vents the borders of race, as her identification with a coloured identity is a shifting effect of the changing landscape of taste, not a solid, immovable object. While
Charmaine sees borders as mobile, Shirley approaches them as flimsy constructs
to be knocked down and exploded. As she deliberately adopts the taste codes of
coloured students, she mocks the rigid world of whites at Fernwood and becomes
a target for hostility. Finally, Zola recognizes the borders, but shys away from them.
Like many African students at Fernwood, she knows the benefits of attending a
formerly white high school, but sees little to be gained from interacting with white,
coloured, or Indian classmates. The borders do not trouble her (at least at the level
of personal interaction), but she has no need to deliberately enter them.

Fernwood students confront the border each day, as they try to carve out
temporary points of affiliation in a setting in which the new is rejected, defied,
and at rare moments, welcomed. Their varying responses to this reality demonstrate that the possible reimaginings of race and identity are multiple: constrained
by history and circumstance, but reinvigorated by the local and global changes
that envelop Fernwood. For the students profiled here, the effort involved in
thinking about and living in border spaces is enormous. As Anne Locke Davidson (1996) reflects, "We no longer live in neatly bounded, homogenous communities, nor do we operate in a purely national economy. For these reasons alone,
the ability to challenge and negotiate social categories can be viewed as an ability worthy of encouragement" (p. 229). Although Davidson writes in the context
of her study of high school students in the United States, her observation is also
applicable to the youth of Fernwood. By choice or chance, Fernwood students are
thrust into the borderlands; their negotiations of these spaces point us towards and
open up multiple futures, including the futures of race.

CHAPTER EIGHT

THE FUTURES OF RACE

Everyone's been so cornered off, everyone was put into a certain topic, you're black, you go there. You're coloured, you go over there. Everybody had a certain class, and now because everything's changed, everybody has just been mushed together, and you have to struggle and find your bearings, and find out where you are in this whole new little nation because before everybody knew their place. A lot of people weren't happy with it, but they knew their place.

-Jackie, white student at Fernwood High

Jackie's comments frame the structuring questions of this book: What happens when, in her words, everyone is "mushed together"? How do youth, who find themselves involuntarily at the forefront of desegregation, think about and live with difference? Jackie's remark that "you have to struggle and find your bearings" speaks to the need for adolescents, and all people, to find places and points of identification, even if they are, as Gils Deleuze and Félix Guattari (1987) argue, temporary points and locations of affiliation.

Fernwood in 1996 is turbulent terrain for this work. Only five years after the first desegregation of white government schools, and two years after the first multiracial elections, one could not describe Fernwood (or South Africa) as "post" apartheid in a sense that suggests that apartheid and its effects have vanished. It is, instead, a "going beyond" (S. Hall, 1996) that incorporates the traces of apartheid and redeploys them in a new conjuncture. Here, there are no necessary

111

outcomes or predetermined paths. Fernwood is one of the sites in which the new, however raw, crude, and unpolished, is formed.

And, in some sense, it is all new. The attitudes of some Fernwood administrators and teachers, formed through years of immersion in apartheid educational and societal systems, sit in a new context and thus resonate a bit differently from before. What was once accepted as common sense is now examined quizzically, interrogated, and perhaps discarded. As a school, Fernwood does not attempt solely to cling to the old, but to refashion and position itself as a particular kind of school (white), within a world that is increasingly black. Its whiteness, assumed and naturalized under apartheid, is no longer. It must struggle to create and solidify this whiteness through its practices and discourses, despite the cost to its predominantly black student population.

With Fernwood as context, this book has analyzed how Fernwood students think about and struggle over difference. Through doing so, I have interrogated fundamental theoretical questions about two central social constructs: race and identity.

THE CONTEXT AND CONTENT OF RACE

"Race" in educational research is often taken as a given, a set, preexisting variable that is then put into conversation with other naturalized states of being, such as gender and class. Despite occasional gestures towards an understanding that race really isn't biological, we still tend to study race as a constant presence, a "fact" of life that unfolds within a predictable, unchanging routine. While we undoubtedly admit to and study change in other aspects of life and work (e.g., education is constantly producing new ideas about teaching and learning), race in educational research is stuck in paradigms that prevent us from putting forward interpretations and analyses that address the staggering complexity of the world in which we find ourselves. As Nicholas Burbules (1997) argues, there exists a "danger that difference can become categorical, static; that we do not rethink particular dimensions of difference as contexts and circumstances change" (p. 109). Race is, without question, a social, not biological fact (Haney Lopez, 1996; Ignatiev, 1995; Omi & Winant, 1994), and part of the job of educational research is to unpack how race functions as a set of practices within schools.

Here, I try to shift the fundamental questions we ask about race to ones that explore its temporal and spatial variability. Instead of assuming what race is, and then proceeding to analyze its effects and manifestations, I engage how race is produced in a particular situation, how it is explained, circulated, and reproduced, and how as a construct it interfaces with various structures of power. In essence, I change the emphasis from drawing and redrawing lines between groups to getting underneath how those lines are produced in the first place and what they mean to people in their everyday lives. As Akhil Gupta and James

Ferguson (1997b) argue in reference to the study of cultural difference, "We are interested less in establishing a dialogic relation between geographically distinct societies than in exploring the processes of production of difference in a world of culturally, socially, and economically interconnected and interdependent spaces" (p. 43). This process of production, in all its complexity, is the focus of my study of Fernwood.

In this book, I have argued that Fernwood students produce race as a discourse of taste. I take seriously and engage with Kris Gutierrez and Peter McLaren's (1995) concern that "educators need to ask themselves how students' identities are organized macrospatially and geopolitically as well as within the micropolitics of the classroom" (p. 128). Identities are not assumed and prefigured, but are shifting constellations that cannot be understood through paradigms that reinscribe them as solid. Furthermore, identities are organized on multiple intersecting planes, both encompassing and creating the scapes (Appardurai, 1996) that structure the contemporary world.

THE LANDSCAPE OF RACE AND TASTE

Racial identity's manifestation as taste functions to reinscribe race as a valid point of suture for students' identities, disrupting and displacing other potential constructions of race, such as nation, culture, or biology. Taste specifically and forcefully organizes itself within what Bourdieu has described as a habitus, a set of practices that assures that structures (such as race) will perpetuate, but never exactly reproduce themselves. Yet as students' engagement with difference at Fernwood moves through taste, race splits open in several ways.

First, the fantasy of race as a purely local construction is shattered, as its embeddedness in the global is made evident. Here, the micropolitics of Fernwood interact with the macrospatial world of global popular culture and inevitably connect to the scapes that reconfigure students' place in the world. By using this approach to my interpretation of the construction of race at Fernwood, I mean to interrupt ethnographic analysis that is narrowly local and sedimented within the bounds of the (ethnographer-invented) traditional village. James Clifford (1997), working against this paradigm, recasts the village as a crossroads, a place of movement or, as he theorizes, a hotel lobby, an urban café, or a bus. He argues, "We often need to consider circuits, not a single place" (p. 37). The circuit, in the case of Fernwood, is broad, encompassing everything from the taxi students take to school to the latest Whitney Houston CD they carry in their book bag as they make the journey. Both the process of their travel to school and the particularity of their affection for Whitney can be analyzed within these scapes that redefine the meaning and impact of these now unbounded circuits.

Second, an analysis based on taste reveals how race functions in multiple, sometimes contradictory, ways. Here, we see how it is possible for not one, but multiple forms of "race" to emerge and function simultaneously. Charting race's course leads in often divergent directions. In Chapter 5, I examined how students use taste to create and police racial borders, defining and enforcing racialized taste codes to separate African, coloured, Indian, and white. Taste codes become an insistent, pounding refrain, managing the minutiae of students' daily lives, and are the structure through which the sociopolitical relations of the school are governed. In this instance, race as a construct retains its power—it does not, of course, exactly replicate, but it uses the logic of the habitus to both reproduce and mutate. But then, in chapter 6, breaks occur in the students' racialized taste practices. Taste, as an affective construct, cannot hold. Alliances develop between groups of students, which, under the strict logics of racialized taste, should be impossible. Taste begins to work with other factors, such as class, to drive and shape, not simply reflect, the constituted racial positionings that students have carefully produced. Taste's dynamism becomes apparent as it is a major factor in cementing relations between coloured and African students in grade 12, and coloured and white students in grade 8. Taste here does not replicate; instead it cracks open, and race falters. How students navigate the racialized borders of Fernwood is the focus of chapter 7, as I deepen and broaden my discussion of race and taste through profiling seven individuals. Taste's role is uneven and, in some stories, muted; yet the strong variability of race emerges through my sketches of the seven students.

THE PLAY OF IDENTITY

Through emphasizing the role of taste in the production of identities, I attempt to destabilize and problematize not only the concept of race, but the very notion of identity itself. Race, of course, is part of this broader problematic that surrounds contemporary social theory and the practices of everyday life. The idea of identity, that everyone "has" one composed of certain components (race, gender, class, nation, ethnicity, etc.) that coalesce or conflict in a particular manner within each individual has its roots in the Enlightenment conception of self (S. Hall, 1992). In this paradigm, an "identity" is solid, unchanging, unfolds through a lifetime, and precedes social forces. Later, of course, this paradigm is rocked by the emergence of the "sociological subject" (S. Hall, 1992) whose identity is formed in constant conversation with the structures of the world. Race, then, is not a necessary category of identity, but one that is created within and becomes salient because of particular historical, economic, and political forms. Through demonstrating how race is formed by taste (and, at moments, how taste forms race), I reveal the instability both of race as a construct, and of identity itself. Identity is at play. Here, I do not use "play" to infer that this process of identity construction is joyful, or that it is a matter of choice, but that it is open to many articulations. In other words, how identity is constituted is not a preordained fact. That identity can be transformed into an affective practice, that of taste, illuminates its variability and complexity. Taste, as I have demonstrated, is not a simple matter.

Applying the construct of taste to identity is not saying that one group wears these clothes and a second group wears another. Instead, it is understanding how taste is produced, how it circulates, how it structures relations, and where and how it falters. The paradigm of taste allows us to see, quite vividly, how identity produces itself. Taste's remarkable instability illuminates the pitfalls of the Enlightenment self—these identities are not stable and preformed, but moving temporary affiliations, ready to alight at any moment.

Taste also underscores the import of affect for identity production. As Grossberg (1989) suggests, popular culture "is intimately implicated in the production of common sense—the multilayered, fragmented collection of meanings, values, and ideas that we both inherit and construct and which largely define our taken-for-granted interpretation of the world" (p. 94). Here, affect becomes part of students' commonsense production of identity, as important and relevant to them as other potential constructions. Stuart Ewen (1988) quotes from a student essay on the topic of style, which mixes reflections on living in a bombed-out building in a Beirut war zone with comments on the popular make of clothing, cars, and contemporary fashion in Beirut. Fernwood students' essays and spoken comments often contain a similar, seemingly bizarre juxtaposition of observations on apartheid and violence and then, without pause, specifics about the racial coding of music and long lists of preferred clothing manufacturers. While I, standing outside their lives, may label apartheid and violence as "important" and clothing as "not so important," it quickly becomes clear that these youth do not share my worldview. I am compelled to recognize that while the remnants of apartheid and violence are forces that bear down on students' lives, popular culture is where students live: where and how they are invested and the raw material they draw on to think about themselves and their relations to others.

RACE, RACISMS, AND EDUCATION

The previous discussion points to the reality that race, and racial identities, are slick and elusive. Race does not proceed unchanged through time and space, but constructs and reconstructs itself, resistant to attempts both to be pinned down and eliminated. Racial identities cannot be bounded and framed, for they exceed, engulf, and mock the borders in which we attempt to encase them. "Racism" does not exist in the singular, as a monolithic, all-encompassing system of domination. Instead, "racisms" (Hall, 1986) proliferate.

Accepting that race and racism are multiple, not singular, constructions raises troubling, probing questions about the design and focus of educational research that investigates these phenomena and other aspects of identity. If we are to understand and intervene in the ways in which race functions within a school setting, it seems imperative that we ask questions about what race is, and how it circulates, reproduces, and changes in that environment. Investigating these questions may lead us to new ways of looking at and thinking about race, and may illuminate spaces of connection that otherwise remain invisible. Here, I follow David Lionel Smith (1998), who in his discussion of black culture argues that "our reliance on 'common sense' racial notions subverts our ability to produce accurate theoretical or even descriptive accounts of our social and cultural circumstances" (p. 181). In this book, I question "common sense" ideas of race, and instead probe critical issues around how and why race is constructed in a specific way at particular time.

For example, by using taste to analyze racialized identities at Fernwood, I am able to interpret the changing landscape of connections and alliances between different racial groups. These alliances (e.g., between African and coloured students in grade 12) may have remained buried or unexplained (and thus ignored) if I neglected to focus on the concerns of taste, popular culture, and a shifting notion of "race." Using these paradigms gives me a new approach, a new way into the racial dynamics of Fernwood.

At the same time, recognizing the multiplicity of race opens up our understanding of the conflicts that dominate Fernwood and many other desegregated schools not just in South Africa, but around the world. Michelle Fine, Lois Weis, and Linda Powell (1997) are concerned with the divisive dynamics that are often found at these sites, and suggest that without an investment in developing community, democratic practices, and ongoing and substantial analysis of the play of "difference, power, and privilege," "settings that are technically desegregated will corrode into sites of oppositional identities, racial tensions, and fractured group relations which simply mirror the larger society" (p. 249). While Fernwood students would likely benefit from the interventions and structural changes suggested by Fine, Weis, and Powell, the story of race and identity at the school suggests that it is important to do in-depth and penetrating analyses of desegregated sites to look for the divergent trajectories of race. The dynamics at Fernwood do not only mirror the larger society (though they do that in some respects), they are, in and of themselves, part of the ongoing conversation and negotiation of race in South Africa and worldwide. If we look at Fernwood in this way, as a productive, not only reflective site, then it becomes a compelling task to study the connections, and the moments and spaces of border crossings and hybridities that exist even without the conditions suggested by Fine, Weis, and Powell. By analyzing the "how" of race, even in instances when it remains a point of conflict and connection, we tease out its complexity. By doing so, we begin with the understandings, connections, and interpretations that students already bring to their engagement with race, and move forward from there. As Grossberg (1994) reflects, "...we must begin where people already are if we want to move them to somewhere else" (p. 99). In the case of Fernwood, students engage with race as a discourse of taste, and through their practices illuminate (often unintentionally) its instability. If "race" was solid, then there would be no crossover in taste preferences, there would be no need to police borders, there would be no alliances or connections. It is only because race is *not* solid that these dynamics exist.

Teaching Race

As the boundaries of racial identities move and shift, they are open to recon-figuration, though in a contextual, not free-floating, manner. As my research and others' (K. Hall, 1995; Maira, 1999; Perry, forthcoming; Wulff, 1995; Yon, 2000) demonstrates, race and racisms are more complex phenomena than our pedagogical practices admit, and we need to move along the road of beginning to engage these complications.

Critically, our pedagogies need to acknowledge the limits of racial iden-tification (McCarthy, 1998) and to focus not on how people are different, but on how such differences are *created* and *sustained* through the culture that sur-rounds us. As Fazal Rizvi (1991) points out in his discussion of ethnicity, "The idea . . . . that ethnic groups maintain their cultural identity is fundamentally ideological" (p. 191). By this, he suggests, with McCarthy, Burbules, and oth-ers, that difference (whether called racial, ethnic, or cultural) is neither natu-ral nor innocent. For example, when a society such as the United States fos-ters and promotes racial/ethnic/cultural difference, it may have the (intended) effect of muting class-based identification.

Thus, instead of sending students on a journey to find out who they are, we need to deepen students' understanding of the "how" and the "why" of difference. This approach would also allow space for engaging with how students themselves (like the students of Fernwood) make sense of "race" and how these meanings are both embedded in, and influence, the structures in which they operate. In other words, instead of insisting that we know in advance what it means to be an "x," and transmitting that to students, we engage in a conversation about that mean-ing and its historical and spatial variability.

In the context of the United States, this might mean talking with both white and black students about how the Irish were (and are still in some con-texts) positioned as black. Stanley Aronowitz (1994) similarly gives the exam-ple of a male youth from Puerto Rico who migrated to the United States in 1929 and "could live through the thirties without being crucially identified as a Puerto Rican—both by himself, by social and economic institutions, and by others" (p. 198). Instead, this young man was both positioned, and positioned himself, pre-dominantly through his class and political identifications. His Puerto Rican "identity" was a small part of his "self" (p. 198), not the overarching racial and/or ethnic position that it is more likely to be today. In South Africa, it might mean examining the racial classifications of apartheid, and how they functioned not only to mark difference, but to actually create and sustain that difference. The pedagogical aim of these practices is to involve students in a project that looks at the ways in which difference is constructed, how its significance shifts, how it is operationalized in a society, and most critically why difference continues to matter. As Burbules (1997) argues, the examination of systems of difference is an integral component of the educational project, and can "illuminate something crucial about the way in which we *make* our lives, in which they are made for us, within tacit categories of sameness or difference that could be re-made differently" (p. 112, emphasis is the author's).

Race, for Fernwood students, is a crucial part of the selves they both inherit and recreate. It is a category of difference that holds enormous power within the historical structures of South African society, and will certainly continue to be a critical point of voluntary and involuntary identification. Despite its tenacity, race is also remade here—sometimes in ways that reinscribe its hold, in other instances, in ways that loosen it. For all of us, the challenge is to dismantle the power of race and difference, so that we are able, in Toni Morrison's (1998) words, to be home.

NEGOTIATING PLACE:

REFLECTIONS ON METHOD, THEORY, AND BEING THERE

In a city built on steep, torturous hills, a car makes all the difference. Getting into my car every morning at 7 or 7:30, I drive out of my neighborhood surrounding the University of Natal, and past dozens of African domestic workers trudging slowly from the bus stops up the hills of Glenwood to the homes of their white employers. The drive from my apartment to Fernwood takes me ten minutes: up the winding roads to the university and then past five of the most prestigious white schools in the area. As I approach the neighborhood surrounding Fernwood, I often spot Fernwood students, those who live close enough to walk to school, start-ing up the massive hill that then plunges into the valley where Fernwood was built. I usually stop to pick up these students, and often similarly transport students home after school or to various bus stops. I am not the only adult at school to do this; many teachers also arrive at school with carloads full of students.

My short and easy journey to school, past the palatial homes of the elite of Durban and then into more modest though almost exclusively white areas, con-trasts sharply with the long, unpleasant daily trip for many Fernwood students. Leaving home at 5:30 or 6 A.M., the majority of African students at Fernwood travel via bus, train, and/or taxi from the townships of Umlazi, to the south, and KwaMashu, to the north—a trip that takes anywhere from one to two hours. The trains, buses, and taxis stop near an industrial and commercial area of Durban, located a fifteen-minute walk from the school. On the rare morning that I drive into school from that direction, I pass hundreds of African students, from both Fernwood and Kingsborough, the school across the highway from Fernwood, streaming from the buses and trains, illegally cutting through holes in the freeway fences and running into the roadway on their way to school.

The differences in our journeys, in the paths we take to get to Fernwood every morning, are consequences of the intertwined global and local political and economic realities that have historically structured anthropological research. Here, I analyze the impact of these contexts, the ways in which my biography intersected with that of Fernwood students, teachers, and other staff, and the implications of these realities for the possibilities for this research.

METHODOLOGICAL CONCERNS AND FRAMES

Methodologically, this research embodies many of the tensions inherent to ethnographic work at the close of the twentieth century. The move into what Yvonna Lincoln and Norman Denzin (1994) refers to as the "fifth moment" requires an acknowledgement of the historical and contemporary realities of colonialism and inequality that have structured encounters between "self" and "other," the problematic "crisis of representation" (Benson, 1993; Clifford & Marcus, 1986; Geertz, 1973; Marcus & Fisher, 1986; Personal Narratives Group, 1989; Rabinow, 1977; Visweswaran, 1994) and a simultaneous reckoning with what Renato Rosaldo (1993) refers to as "an interdependent late twentieth-century world" (p. 217) that merits study and investigation, including ethnographic inquiry.

I move beyond naturalistic ethnographic methods that concern themselves with uncovering a reality situated in the emic perspective of the research participants (Roman, 1993). It is impossible to access such a position, nor, does one pure emic position exist. Instead, the analysis presented here is the result of the conversations that emerged from the dialogic relations (Denzin, 1995) of the field. In this vein, I am influenced by interpretive methodologies that locate the process of the creation of textuality in the interstice between myself and others. The worlds that qualitative researchers analyze are not discovered, but created in the texts we write (Denzin, 1995). Here, I am cognizant, as Peter McLaren (1992) argues, that these relations and practices are "entangled within larger structures of power and privilege" (p. 78). While I am sympathetic to ethnographic efforts (e.g., Behar, 1993) that attempt to forefront the ways in which these structures weave through the work of anthropologists and ethnographers, in this text I decide to interpret the lives of Fernwood students, understanding that the stories and truths I could tell are multiple (Lather, 1991). As will be apparent through the following sections of this appendix, my story is crucial to my experiences in the field, and the resulting tale can be read as a slice of the negotiation of identity and relations between people in a inextricably enmeshed, though unequal, world (Enslin, 1994; Fine,

1994). Partiality, perspective, and position are understood as frames that enable, not strangle, the role of research in both interpreting and affecting the world.

BEGINNINGS

Teachers at Fernwood have regular parking spots. Not wanting to infringe on their routines, I end up parking, every day, at the end of a line of cars bordering the driveway to the school, behind a small, battered, red car with a Natal rugby bumpersticker. Every morning, after parking my car, I am confronted with one of the daily dilemmas of an ethnography of this type—where to now? It's 7:30, about fifteen minutes before the first bell rings, and students and teachers are scattered all over the school. On my way into the driveway I passed a few prefects standing at the gate, and a group of white students sitting, as they do every morning, on the set of stairs leading from the driveway down to the field. They guard their space ferociously. According to school rules that area is off bounds to all students, yet the white students consider it theirs, and I have heard about clashes with black students who try to sit on the stairs. Only matrics are allowed on the driveway; the majority of students must stay on the expansive field next to the school building until the bell rings. On winter mornings, which can be quite chilly in the valley where Fernwood is located, students huddle together and near the toilets to stay warm, wearing gloves, hats, and sweaters. The prefects' room is the warmest room at the school during the winter, and many of the prefects routinely neglect their duties and gather there to talk and do their homework. As there is no early morning teacher's meeting at Fernwood anymore (it has been replaced this year with meetings twice a week during tea break—the first break of the day) teachers socialize in the teachers' lounge, sit in their classrooms preparing for the day, grab a smoke in the teachers' smoking room, or do field duty. The cleaning staff is often busy cleaning and resetting the hall after an outside function from the night before, and Regina, the "tea lady," starts on her first round of the day, delivering tea directly to the individual offices of the management, and setting out the cups, saucers, and tea urn for the rest of the teachers.

When I first arrived at Fernwood in February 1996, these routines were foreign to me. My only previous experience of South African schooling had been in 1995 when I spent two months visiting ten schools in Durban, including Fernwood, in anticipation of this research. School uniforms, prefects, formal school assemblies, rugby, daily tea service and a school tea lady, students standing and greeting teachers when they entered a classroom, and strict rules and hierarchies were far removed from my years in a 99% white, middle and working-class, suburban Boston high school. I had to continually remind myself that many students and teachers at Fernwood concurred that it was a casual, relaxed and friendly school compared to other schools (white or Model C, African, coloured, and Indian) in the Durban area. While it is also true that there was a sizable group of teachers interested in making the school more democratic, eliminating uniforms, and changing the formal nature of the school, overall it was abundantly clear that I came to Fernwood with a different set of experiences and theoretical investments than many of the students and staff.

I first visited South Africa in 1992, after years of involvement in the divestment movement and a U.S.-based foundation that raised funds for the anti-apartheid movement within South Africa. My interests in race and identity drew me back several times, and eventually led to this research in 1996. My first visit to Durban was in 1995 and consisted of a two-month stay in Chatsworth, the Indian township where my then-partner (now husband) grew up and where his family still lives. During this time, I arranged short visits to approximately ten high schools in the Durban area, so as to be able to select one for my research the following year. I chose Fernwood High as my research site, over several other schools, for two reasons. First, Fernwood in 1996 was the most racially integrated school in Durban, thus providing the most appropriate site for the study of racial identity in a multiracial environment. In making the decision to conduct my study at Fernwood, I realized that my research questions could not be easily answered at a typical or representative school with a decidedly more racially homogenous student body. I employed a logic used by Robert Stake (1995) when he argues for the value of what he terms an "instrumental" case study. In an instrumental case study, the researcher has particular questions in mind, (in my case about racial identity in a multiracial context) and then looks for the situation in which one can learn the most about the issue at hand. Stake argues that "sometimes a 'typical' case works well but often an unusual case helps illustrate matters we overlook in typical cases" (p. 4). Given my specific interest in how racial identity is negotiated in a multiracial environment, it was necessary that I choose a school that was atypical, at least for Durban, at the moment of this research.

In addition to this theoretical concern, there was a practical aspect to my decision as well. Fernwood, unlike other schools in Durban, was somewhat accustomed to the presence of researchers and journalists and was willing to give me free and unrestricted access to the school. As there is little history of ethnographic, school-based research in South Africa, I was concerned that other schools, though eager at the beginning, may not have been entirely aware of the implications of having a researcher in their school on a daily basis for a year. For example, several principals I met with at other schools were overly excited about my request for an initial visit and quickly agreed to everything I asked, without question or thought. Realizing this response may have been politeness to a visitor from the United States and/or inexperience, I opted for Fernwood.

However, to provide some perspective on Fernwood, I spent short amounts of time (usually three to five days) at three other schools: an Indian school, a coloured school, and Kingsborough High, an African high school (with a multiracial teaching staff and predominantly white administration) located across the highway from Fernwood. Additionally, I simultaneously collected data in two history classes at two other Model C, all girls high schools. Finally, on a monthly basis I met with a group of students involved with a youth organization in Durban. These five students, from high schools throughout the metropolitan area, provided me with additional checks on the data collected at Fernwood and contacts with students outside Fernwood.

Michael Green, one of the deputy vice-principals at Fernwood and a former lecturer at the University of Natal–Durban, facilitated my access to Fernwood, and secured me an empty office next to the school guidance counselor. Although this space never fully evolved into a drop-in place for students because of the ways in which their movements were tightly controlled (i.e., the school building was off-bounds to students before and after school and during breaks), there still were moments when students would pass by, stop, and talk. I also used the office for interviewing, study sessions, group discussions, and, on a few occasions, for counseling a student.

ENTERING FERNWOOD

During my first few months at the school, I obtained permission to attend several English classes on a regular basis. Most of the teaching at Fernwood in 1996 was still lecture and teacher centered, a system driven both by tradition and a rigid internal and provincial exam system. Thus, classes generally were not the most productive spaces for the generation of data, except on the occasions when teachers would be ill or busy and I could sit and talk to students. Over the course of the year, my class attendance was focused on these specific English classes, though I also visited, on at least one occasion, most of the teachers' classrooms.

In the early months, I steadfastly avoided extended contact with teachers and situations in which I would be taking the place of a teacher: substituting, administering a test, or in any other way performing duties normally associated with a teacher. Although it was not an unproblematic decision, I was deeply concerned about the strict hierarchical nature of the system, the tensions and mistrust between students and teachers at Fernwood, and the ways in which South African children are socialized to treat adults. I could not afford to be seen or treated like a teacher.

However, respecting the conventions of the school, it was necessary for me to dress rather conservatively. My lack of a uniform marked me within the school as a teacher; it was vital for the research to minimize, in other ways, that affiliation. I could never, in any way, "blend in" with students, nor could I ever, even in passing, be mistaken for a student by a teacher. I was also, of course, not subject to the same rules as students, being free to come and go from school and generally create my own schedule, while still respecting the school's. For example, I never entered a class late or left early, conformed as much as possible to school rules, and was generally constantly conscious that I was there as a guest of Fernwood, not as a friend of the students with whom I spent most of my time. Given these restrictions and circumstances, I cannot, and do not claim, that my experience in any way approximated that of a Fernwood student or teacher. Early in the research, I did attempt to establish a small, discussion-based class for grade 11 students (because matric students are tightly bound to their classes in preparation for the provincial exams at year-end) about democracy and change in South Africa. However, scheduling became problematic as students' study and civic periods gradually became testing periods and the class disintegrated. In the end, I interacted with Fernwood primarily as an observer. Participation in any of the already constituted categories existing at the school was not possible.

MAKING FRIENDS?

The process of building trust with students took months and did not crystalize until they realized, as Nikki told me much later, that I was not going to repeat anything they said to the teachers. My earliest relations were with a subset of the prefect group. While this may seem, and in some ways is, an elite group, several factors contributed to this choice. First and most centrally, prefects are one of the only racially integrated student groups at Fernwood and the only group functioning that way on a daily basis (i.e., the basketball team is racially integrated, but they do not function as a team in the school on a daily basis, but resegregate). The prefects were perhaps the only possible base I could establish within the school to meet students from different racial groups. Any other choice of a "home base" would have meant picking one racial group and, by default, eliminating any possibility of friendships with the other racial groups. This was not my original reason for meeting the prefects before other students, yet I rapidly realized that compared to other segments of the school, racial contact that generated both conflict and connection was highest among this group. Yet, as should be apparent from the research presented, there was no manufactured harmony or romantic nonracialism operating among this group; relations between prefects were dominated by the politics and divides of race.

Second, and critically at least at the beginning of this study, prefects had a modicum of freedom of movement not allowed to other students, making them a generally more accessible group. Although I was to learn later that this was due to the administration's lax supervision, I had easy access to a group of prefects who would gather, for example, during a study lesson in their office, whereas access to other students was much more limited, formal, and controlled by teachers.

Despite the aura surrounding prefects at other schools, Fernwood prefects are not held in such esteem and thus my relationships with them did not negatively affect my relations with other matrics. Instead, my friendship with one prefect would then ease my relationship with a whole group (usually racially exclusive) of their friends. Prefects at Fernwood do not see themselves and are not regarded as model students, despite the efforts of the teachers to construct them in such a fashion. However, as the year waned, prefects were more likely than other matrics to show up for school, which was clearly important for the continuity of the research.

Later in the year after the matrics started their exams, I did form closer relations with some of the younger students: The relations I had built with older students, many of whom are cousins or siblings of the younger students, facilitated a level of trust that I could not have built initially, given the previously discussed hierarchies of South African schooling. Although I was honest with the students about my age (thirty-one at the time—older than a good percentage of the teachers), they insisted on thinking I was in my early twenties. Because in their eyes I did not act like their teachers, I successfully, in most cases, created an adult identity and presence that was not marked by the attributes of "teacher."

Particular moments outside of the classroom also cemented my relations with students. For example, about one month after I began the research, the school held a Debs' ball, discussed in chapter 6. As I danced and talked with students for the first time in an informal atmosphere, and was pushed into the middle of a dance circle to their cheers, I crossed particular lines that teachers at the school did not: Through my practices I consciously separated myself from those constraints. The following Monday in school, many students commented on my presence at the dance, and smiled and talked to me for the first time. Similarly, early in the research I spent a Saturday with Fernwood students at a coloured disco in town, and this news traveled rapidly around the school. There were occasions when students tried to manipulate me and exploit my interest in them for their own benefit: most notably, I was infrequently asked to provide a "cover story" for parents so that they could go out at night to a disco or sneak off with a boyfriend. These requests were always denied—I explained that if anything happened to them, and I had lied, I would most likely be asked to leave the school. Students seemed to respect my answer or, at least, if they persisted in using me as an alibi, I was not informed.

THE POLITICS AND PRACTICES OF RACE, GENDER, AND PLACE

Race, as constructed under apartheid and deployed as a political, economic, and social system, informed many of my experiences in South Africa. It defined, in large measure, where I lived while conducting my research, as the neighborhoods within reasonable commuting distance of Fernwood were predominantly white. As a white I certainly benefited from the privileges of whiteness (McIntosh, 1988), though within the boundaries of Fernwood my race was sometimes ambiguous and shifting. With dark, thick, curly hair, dark features, and a skin tone closer to the world of the Mediterranean and the Middle East than the "whiteness" portrayed on American television, my racial identity, within Fernwood, was not automatically assumed. As students told me many months later, some thought I was white, and others, slotting me into South African racial categories, thought I was coloured. Unaware of the differences between South African and U.S. racial categorization, some students assumed that I was a coloured in the United States. The ambiguity was compounded by the fact that I did not, as some students commented, "act white."

For example, many students knew and had met my partner, Stephen, who is Indian South African. It is unclear if this knowledge dramatically affected what students would say to me (see, e.g., chapter 6, note 4). One white student, who had met Stephen, would denounce Indians as cheats and simultaneously insist that Stephen and I join her and her boyfriend for a night out. A coloured student, Nikki, who met Stephen several times, made derogatory remarks about Indians during our taped interview, and then, embarrassed, said, "Don't tell Stephen I said that!" She did not, however, change or modify what she had said. Her racial stereotyping co-exists, and it appears not uncomfortably, with her lived experience.

Perhaps because of the somewhat ambiguous nature of my racial identity, I was easily accepted by coloured students at Fernwood. I do not mean to imply that I was seen as coloured as many examples made it clear that I was not. But the slight degree of uncertainty and my initial racial coding deeply affected the relations I would subsequently build with students at Fernwood and ultimately the story that I can tell. Of the racial groups at Fernwood, white students were consistently the most difficult for me to form friendships with—they were the most distant and untrusting. Perhaps, even though they saw me as white, they disapproved of my alliances with coloured and African students. Or, as the racial group that views itself as the most threatened at Fernwood, they may simply have been unfriendly to anyone who is an outsider, particularly a person with questions about race and desegregation. Finally, my relationships with students were also influenced by the particular racial dynamics within their subgroups. At the matric level, coloured and African girls were friends, and it was thus relatively easy to move in those circles. However, at the younger levels of the school, coloured students had closer ties with whites, allowing me to move more smoothly along that path.

The gender relations of the school and my positioning within them also shaped the research. Fernwood is only one of two coed white high schools in Durban, the other being a technical school with a small female population. Despite many students', particularly girls', insistence that they came to Fernwood because it was coed, and they did not like the "catty, snobby" girls of the all-girls schools, friendship groups were often gender segregated. With a few limited exceptions, primarily among the older white students, the territory of school was marked by gender just as much as race. As a woman, entrée into girls' groups and conversations in and out of class was fairly easy—they were always eager to talk about the boys they liked, discuss their dresses for the matric dance, ask questions about sex, and repeatedly inquire about my partner (boyfriend in their terms), when we were getting married, if I had picked out a wedding dress, and when we were having children. These girls' questions and priorities also highlighted some of the class differences that existed between myself and many of the students. Raised in a middle-class family in a Boston suburb, I was expected to go to college and begin a career before considering marriage and children. As a high school student, marriage, weddings, and children were never a concern. In contrast, the girls at Fernwood (in the upper grades, particularly the white girls), who are generally from families with less economic and educational privilege than mine, were deeply invested in traditional female roles and had few concrete career plans. Most expected to work or attend technikon for a few years after high school graduation, but rather quickly get married and have children. The female students who were more interested in going to university and having a career were generally African and Indian students from middle-class families, a relatively small percentage of Fernwood students.

In contrast to girls, large groups of boys proved more formidable. They would stop talking if I approached and became noticeably more self-conscious. Gender, compounded by age, separated me from many of the boys in the school. I did form some individual friendships with boys, often those not affiliated with these larger groups and during the second half of the year, some close relationships with boys who were part of gender mixed groups in the lower grades. However, in broad strokes, my key informants and closest friends in the school were coloured girls, followed equally by African and white girls (and I was on good terms with the small number of Indian girls in the upper grades). Thus, though in my interviews I attempted to achieve gender balance, my daily experiences at the school were filtered through the lenses of the girls: It is their reality—from the girls' toilets, to sitting with them in a gender-segregated school assembly, to passing out pads and tampons to girls too shy to go to the school secretary—that structures much of the ethnographic data I collected. As Michael Jackson (1989) argues, ethnographers' stories are "grounded in our practical, personal, and participatory experience in the field as much as our detached observations" (p. 3).

My positioning within the school as the "American visitor" also shaped the possibilities for this research. At the beginning of the research, many students interacted with me through a persona that they had created in the global space of cultural flows. American popular culture was the first and the most important topic that Fernwood students wanted to discuss with me. Questions about which movie stars I knew and how many I had seen dominated initial interactions. I would sometimes be randomly stopped in the hallways of Fernwood by a student I did not know who wanted to ask me for the mailing address of a movie star or a basketball player. And significantly, on my return to the United States in December I carried with me five letters from Fernwood students to Oprah Winfrey—the only thing I was asked to take back with me. While one or two Fernwood students had been to the United States, and more had relatives who had traveled there, for the majority their only experience of my "home" was through the global popular.

Unfortunately, I disappointed many students. I could not provide them with the intimate knowledge of the neighborhoods (South Central L.A., Brooklyn), hip-hop culture, and basketball stars that to them represent the United States. I am not implying that an African-American would, necessarily, bring them this information or that another white could not have filled this role. But, from many students' perspective, I lacked the authenticity of a "real American," which for them is defined through their exposure to sports and popular culture. Indeed, Fernwood students were more familiar with particular aspects of American popular culture than I was—they were often teaching me about a world I may physically but not imaginatively inhabit. I was not, then, a bridge across cultural and spatial difference (Gupta & Ferguson, 1992) in any traditional anthropological sense. It is abundantly clear that such sharp demarcations are not possible.

Just as Fernwood students viewed me through a particular lens, I had similarly initially constructed them through my knowledge of South Africa from outside the country, and from my world of political and academic contacts. For example, I had initially prefigured that discourses such as the rainbow nation and the new South Africa would have meaning for these students as they were prominent ways in which South Africa was discursively constructed. My investment in and construction of South Africa had very little to do with the everyday lives of these South African children, just as their construction of "Americans" had little to do with mine.

Although the United States was the imaginary center of the world for many students, particularly African and coloured students, there was little realization on their part that the flow of images and commodities between the United States and South Africa is predominantly one-way. This assumption of an equal exchange was reflected in the questions students would ask me: for example, I would often be asked what American teenagers thought about South African teenagers, which South African television programs were broadcast in the United States, and which South African musical groups were popular there. Several students expressed surprise and confusion that I did not know Afrikaans, assuming that I would have learned at least enough of the language to follow the South African Afrikaans news, which they thought was broadcast in the United States. There was continual frustration expressed that "we know so much about American teenagers, why don't they know anything about us," which reveals that while South African teenagers may be voracious consumers of U.S. popular culture, they are not fully informed of the geopolitics surrounding their practices of consumption.

RELATIONS WITH TEACHERS

As my relationships with students became more secure, I also slowly began to venture into the staff room on a more regular basis, an area which was off-limits to students. I was constantly aware in those moments of walking through the door that represented the line that no students, including prefects, were allowed to cross, of the multiple ways in which I had to straddle and cross borders to accomplish this research. In a school dominated by tense, strained, and sometimes hostile relations between students and staff, deciding which side to be on was a constant struggle. Over time, I believe that most of the teachers began to see me as predominantly on the student side—though I had to reexplain continually that I was at Fernwood to research students' lives and thus it was important for me to spend time with them. This splitting occurred often at school functions, when I was frequently asked, "Don't you want to sit with the teachers?" and I had to gently insist, that no, I wanted to sit with the students. My position was tenuous and I was scrupulously aware of the dangers inherent in my splitting. I realized that if anything confidential discussed in teachers' meetings somehow got to the students, I would be the first to be blamed—thus, I was on guard to maintain strict confidentiality on both sides.

Unlike students, teachers seemed less concerned about my racial identity, accepting me as white. They were more interested in my positioning as an American, though from a decidedly different perspective than the students. Teachers often asked me questions about how things were done in schools in the United States, told me about their travels to the United States, complained about the exchange rate, and one teacher, a geology buff, quizzed me incessantly about rocks. But generally for the teachers, who were 95% white, the United States was not a major point of interest or investment. New Zealand, Australia, England, and Singapore captured their imagination and, for many, offered a realistic way out of a South Africa that they no longer wanted to live in.

My experiences with teachers were more significantly marked by the politics of gender and age. For many of the management and the older male teachers, I was, primarily because of my gender and age, invisible. Although I had been introduced to the staff formally and by the middle of the year knew almost all of them, many of the older males on staff would still ask me how the honours (in South Africa, the fourth, optional year of an undergraduate degree) was going. They were still surprised when I explained, again, that I was doing Ph.D. research. Although I deliberately dressed and acted conservatively and appropriately (as the other female teachers), I was still, overall, not respected as a serious researcher by the preponderance of men on staff.

My relations with female teachers were also marked and divided by age. I had friendly relations with all of the younger women teachers, yet the older women, with a few exceptions, were curt and distant. For the older women and men on staff, the changes at Fernwood, and in South African schooling in general, were coming towards the middle or end of long careers. For those too young to retire, too scared (and, often, too racist) to stay, and too old to move to another country, the chaos of Fernwood in 1996 was profoundly traumatic. For them, those who were cursing change at least on the local level of the school, my research was threatening, strange, and, ultimately, irrelevant to their lives.

METHOD IN THE FIELD

The data represented in this research are based on participant-observation for approximately four (often five) days per week at Fernwood for the period

March–December 1996. I attempted to schedule my visits to other Durban schools during Fernwood exams period, though I sometimes left Fernwood for a few hours in the middle of the day for short visits to other neighboring schools. In addition, I attended school functions on the nights and weekends, including sporting events, dances, the school fashion show, prizegiving occasions and presentations, parents' meetings, governing board meetings, and social events with teachers. I also spent time informally outside of school with numerous students, going to the beach, shopping, out to lunch, to the movies, just hanging out, and, on occasion, to a disco. I established strong friendships with several girls, and spoke to them on the phone both during the week and on the weekends. Field notes were recorded on a daily basis.

Taped interviews were conducted with forty five students, mostly individually, but particularly with the younger students also in groups of two. In selecting students for interviews, I tried to achieve some measure of gender and race balance, and to interview students from different peer groups. However, I also interviewed all the students with whom I spent a considerable amount of time, so coloured students are statistically overrepresented in my samples. As the study concentrated on matric students, the majority of interviews are from this cohort, though I also included some younger students. The interviews were semistructured, with a flexible interview protocol developed through the early months of the research. The interviews were generally short (thirty to forty minutes), as I normally had to fit them in before school, or at lunchtime, though occasionally I was allowed to take a student out of a study period for an interview. After school was a difficult time for students, as most either worked or had sports practice. When necessary, I followed up with students whose interviews were incomplete, though usually in casual conversation. The questions I asked revolved around their reactions to discourses such as the new South Africa and the rainbow nation, their experiences at a multiracial school, their understandings of race, racial identity, racial relations at the school, their views on the changes taking place in South Africa, and their plans for the future (see protocol). Furthermore, fifty three students in two English classes that I attended on a regular basis (grade 11 and grade 12) were assigned an essay entitled "How I see myself in terms of my race, culture, nation and individual identity" as part of my research. The essay assignment, which was designed by the teacher with my input, was one of the students' regular, graded writing projects for the term, though students were aware that I would be using their essays as part of my research and that they would be identified by pseudonyms. Many students expressed that they enjoyed the assignment because it was more engaging than their usual essay topics, and many offered to do followup interviews with me.

During the year, I also conducted informal, usually untaped, interviews with at least fifteen groups of five to twelve students. This number includes group interviews I conducted at the other schools I visited, and monthly meetings with the group of five students from the Durban-wide youth organization. I also interviewed twenty three of twenty nine Fernwood teachers and management: for most of these interviews I took notes, but also taped several of them. The questions I asked teachers generally encompassed their personal history at the school, their experiences of change, their analysis of the current situation, and their perspective on the future (see protocol). I did not formally interview any parents (except for the chair of the governing body, also a parent), yet I had numerous informal conversations with parents of all races, and got to know several students' parents well.

Interview Protocol—students: Sample Questions

1. Fernwood is sometimes referred to as a school that is representative of "the rainbow nation." What do you think of this description?
2. Tell me about the differences (if any) you see between students at Fernwood.
3. How would you describe those differences?
4. How would you describe your own racial/cultural background?
5. Tell me about how the different racial/cultural groups interact at Fernwood.
6. Tell me what it's like to be a student at Fernwood.
7. What have been your experiences at Fernwood with students from different racial and/or cultural backgrounds than your own?
8. What's the best thing about Fernwood?
9. What's the worst thing about Fernwood?
10. If you were headmaster of Fernwood, what, if anything, would you change about the school?
11. What do you do when you're not in school?
12. Do you interact with students from different racial and/or cultural backgrounds outside of school? If so, where and how?
13. I often hear the phrase the "new South Africa." What, if anything, do you think is new about South Africa?
14. What, if anything, has changed in your life because of the "new South Africa"?
15. What's the best thing about the new South Africa?
16. What's the worst or most difficult thing about the new South Africa?
17. What are your plans for the future?
18. What do you think South Africa will be like in five years, in ten?

Interview Protocol—teachers and Management: Sample Questions

1. How long have you been teaching at Fernwood?
2. What factors led to your coming here?
3. How would you describe Fernwood to someone who has never been here before?

4. What do you think are the school's strengths?

5. What do you see as Fernwood's major challenges over the next five years?

6. How would you characterize relations between the staff and students?

7. How would you characterize relations between the students?

8. What effect, if any, do the relations between students (specifically racial relations) have on the school as a whole?

9. How would you describe Fernwood's identity?

10. If you were headmaster of Fernwood, what, if anything, would you change?

11. What do you think Fernwood will be like in five years, in ten?

12. Five years from now, will you still be here?

13. What are your plans for the future?

14. What do you think South Africa will be like in five years, in ten?

NOTES

CHAPTER ONE

1. Under apartheid, individuals were assigned one of four population categories: African, Indian, coloured, or white. With the rise of black consciousness in the 1970s, "black" came to symbolize the shared oppression of Africans, Indians, and coloureds. Some of the complexities of racial categorization will be discussed in chapter 2. For my purposes in this book, "black" will be used as an overarching term for Africans, Indians, and coloureds. However, because the specific identifications from the apartheid-era still have meaning and resonance for Fernwood students (though, as I argue, their meanings are not mere replications of apartheid), the categories of African, Indian, and coloured will be used as necessary to demonstrate the ways in which they still structure daily life. That said, "black" in common usage in South Africa is equivalent to African, and should be read that way in quotes from Fernwood students and staff.

2. The statistics on the racial composition of Fernwood are my estimates based on observation. The school did not keep official (at least public, official) statistics on racial composition in 1996.

3. For a qualitative study in the Australian context that takes a similar theoretical approach to race see Rizvi (1993).

4. For example, Proweller (1998, p. 236) specifically excludes the context of popular culture as a factor in her analysis of girls' identities. While I do not mean to critique her bracketing of the popular (as I have similarly bracketed different factors), her study is typical in its exclusion of popular culture as a site of analysis.

5. Exceptions include some of the literature on popular culture and literacy (i.e., Dyson, 1997), and a growing field of scholarship that explicitly examines the influence of popular culture on identity (Mazzarella & Pecora, 1999; McCarthy, Hudak, Miklaucic, & Saukko, 1999; Walkerdine, 1997).

CHAPTER TWO

1. See Johnstone (1976) on job color bars in the mining industry.

2. This is a rather crude division; a specific place in the hierarchy does not necessarily correspond to a particular economic location. For example, there were/are Indians

who lived more destitute lives than Africans, and some Africans who were/are wealthier than whites. On nonsynchrony in racial/class locations, see Buroway (1981), Marks
and Trapido (1987), and McCarthy (1990).

3.   There is an extensive literature on the education of black South Africans from a range
of perspectives. Kallaway, Kallaway, and Sheward (1986) list 4,000 books, theses, conference proceedings, government publications, and journal and newspaper articles.

4.   Although religious education had been eliminated at Fernwood in 1995 because of
budget cutbacks, Christian prayer was the only type of religious expression permitted
at school assemblies and other functions.

5.   Unterhalter (1991) notes one instance in which African primary schooling was compulsory: in Department of Education and Training (nonbantustan) areas, by voluntary local option. This policy affected only 4.7% of African primary-school children
(South African Institute of Race Relations 1989, p. 259).

6.   The term "open schools" in the South African context should in no way be confused
with the "open schools" movement in Britain and the United States, which stressed stu-
dent-centered pedagogy. "Open schools" in South Africa came to mean simply schools
that were open to all racially demarcated groups. No changes in pedagogy or curriculum
were implied by the terms, though this was an issue of contention early on. For a complete discussion of the history of open schools in South Africa, see Christie (1990).

7.   In 1988, for example, there were 233,910 students enrolled in Indian schools; 832,329
students in coloured schools; 935,903 students in white schools; and 7,027,573 students in African schools. The figure for African schools includes African schools in
white-designated areas, in the non-independent homelands (or bantustans), and in
the "independent" homelands. At the time, statistics were kept separately (South
African Institute of Race Relations, 1990, p. 814).

8.   For example, it is only in 1999 that the South African Human Rights Commission
issues a report on race, racial relations, and desegregation in schools. See Vally and
Dalamba (1999).

CHAPTER THREE

1.   Statistics from 1996 South African government census. Retrieved at
http://www.statssa.gov.za/census96.

CHAPTER FOUR

1.   In my discussion of the management and teachers' construction of race, I use "black"
as coterminous with African. I make this exception here (and only here) because management and teachers' construction of "black" applies only to African students. The
number of coloured and Indian students is in general too small for concern or focus.

2.   For literature that specifically addresses white South African identities, see Behr, 1995;
Crapanzano, 1985; R. W. Johnson, 1996; McGurk, 1990; J. Richards, 1996; Steyn,
1996; Van Rooyen, 1994.

3. Rugby also has a distinct Afrikaner history in South Africa. For a discussion of this and other issues regarding sports and identity in South Africa, see Bose, 1994; Farred, 1997; Grundlingh, Odendall, and Spies, 1995; "Issues of rugby and race," 1996; Kirk, 1996; and Steenvald and Sterlitz, 1998.

4. Although the issue of academic standards is occasionally publicly addressed (particularly after dismal midyear results), the administration does not use academic achievement as a significant site of school identity. If it did, it would have to acknowledge that, on the whole, black students were more academically motivated and successful than whites.

5. The prefect system in South African schools is a remnant of British empire. Prefects are selected by management from among the grade 12 students, and are captained by a "head girl" and "head boy"—each responsible for the prefects of their gender. In theory, prefects are responsible for maintaining and administering discipline in schools—historically this includes administering corporeal punishment. At Fernwood, the prefect system is rather weak; though prefects can and do administer punishments (such as writing essays and running an all-school detention), most students pay little attention to them, and most prefects are not overly concerned with their duties. For example, during the all-school detention (held in the school hall), many students left early en masse, and the prefects had no way to stop or discipline them. At this detention, many prefects were also more concerned with getting out of school than they were with enforcing discipline.

CHAPTER FIVE

1. The approach I take here to analyzing African students' identities resonates with Kwaku Korang's (1999) call for a "worldly approach that makes self and other coeval, not an ethnic approach that confines otherness in a prison-house of difference" (p. 30). Throughout this book, I emphasize the coevalness (which does not imply absolute equality) of Fernwood students of all racialized backgrounds, and that they meet and negotiate identities through the common practices of popular culture.

2. For extended discussion of consumption and identity, also see Howes (1996) and P. Jackson (1993). For an overview of the literature, see Dant (1999) and MacKay (1997).

3. A shared taste, however, does not necessarily always translate into a shared identity. For example, see my portrait of Jackie (chapter 7), and Grossberg (1992).

4. Taxis, known as vans in the United States, are the primary form of transportation for the majority of (black) people. Taxis are privately owned, overcrowded, often poorly maintained, and usually driven at excessive speeds to minimize time and maximize profits. Taxis are responsible for the majority of highway deaths in South Africa each year. By the late 1990s, there were new initiatives to regulate the taxi industry.

    Taxis, and taxi culture, are extremely youth-oriented. Taxis market themselves to youth through the particular music they play (at ear-splitting decibels) and the reputation of the driver. Fernwood students often choose their taxi by these criteria, with the roster of "in" and "out" taxis changing frequently.

5. Amanda's "racial" identity is complex, as I will discuss in chapter 7. I identify her here (and in most places throughout the book) as coloured. Despite her Indian background,

she does not consciously and publicly self-identify as Indian within Fernwood (perhaps for reasons discussed in chapter 2), and while she is also is identified as "white" and "black" (here meaning African) on occasion, in this quote she tries to speak to the meaning of "coloured" from an insider perspective, however problematic that position may be.

6. Because of the very small number of Indian students at Fernwood in 1996, I cannot adequately discuss and analyze a distinct Indian racialized identity that is constructed through clothing. The few Indian students at Fernwood tend to gravitate towards the coloured style and identity, and thus I will discuss them in tandem with coloured students.

7. R50 was equivalent to U.S. $11 or $12 at 1996 exchange rates and was considered extremely inexpensive for jeans. In contrast, Levis ranged from R250 to 400, and the jeans preferred by African students, such as Giorgio Armani, ranged from R500 to 1000.

8. The "toyi-toyi" is a practice associated with black political protest. While not exactly a dance, it incorporates repetitive physical movements that are distinctive and easily recognizable. Janice explains the toyi-toyi in terms that are familiar to her, hence, she thinks of it as a dance.

CHAPTER SIX

1. The Group Areas Act gave the government the authority to segregate South Africa by allocating separate areas to demarcated racial groups. The implementation of this policy led to widespread forced removals, and disrupted the lives of millions of (mainly black) people. The act was passed in 1950 and repealed in 1991, though of course its legal repeal has had (to date) only minimal effect on reversing racial segregation of the population.

2. "Kaffir" is a derogatory term for an African person.

3. "Coolie" is a derogatory term for an Indian person. Although Janice, like many students (of all racialized identities) may be confused about the term. As "coolie" sounds like/is close to "coloured," some of the students use it to refer to coloured students, unaware of its historical trajectory. I was sometimes asked to clarify this (students do find their uses for "experts" on race—this was something I should know) The student in question, Melissa, is of mixed coloured and Indian background.

4. Nikki's hesitation, and her addition of "Well, it's not not right," may reflect her belated realization that her comments might have been offending me as my partner (whom she had met on numerous occasions) is Indian and I am white. For more on my racialized identity within the school, see the appendix.

5. The use of the word "nation" here must be understood in its South African context. Under apartheid, the government often referred to the demarcated population groups as "nations," which existed either inside of (in the case of African) or within but separate from (in the case of Indians and coloureds) the South African nation, which was white. The Bantu Homelands Citizenship Act, passed in 1970, attempted to create separate "nations" (commonly known as bantustans or homelands) for the multiple (sometimes created or recreated) African ethnic groups, thereby making them foreigners in South Africa, under South African law. No nation-state in the world rec-

ognized these "nations" except for South Africa. The use of "nation" to describe different racialized groups lingers in the South African vocabulary.

CHAPTER SEVEN

1. The portrait of Jackie is an illustration of Grossberg's analysis of taste. See chapter 5, note 2.

REFERENCES

Adam, H. (1995). The politics of ethnic identity: Comparing South Africa, *Ethnic and Racial Studies* 18(3), 457–475.

Allinson, E. (1994). It's a black thing: Hearing how whites can't. *Cultural Studies*, 8 (3), 438–456.

Altbach, P., & Kelly, G. (Eds.). (1984). *Education and the colonial experience* (2nd Rev. ed). New Brunswick, NJ: Transaction.

Anderson, B. (1991). *Imagined communities: Reflections on the origin and spread of nationalism*. London: Verso.

Anzaldúa, G. (1987). *Borderlands/La Frontera*. San Francisco: Aunt Lute Books.

Anzaldúa, G., & Hernandez, E. (1995/1996), Re-thinking margins and borders: An interview. *Discourse* 18(1&2), 7–15.

Appadurai, A. (1990) Disjuncture and difference in the global cultural economy. *Public Culture* 2(2), 1–24.

Appadurai, A. (1996). *Modernity at large: Cultural dimensions of globalization*. Minneapolis: University of Minnesota Press.

Aronowitz, S. (1994). *Dead artists, live theories and other cultural problems*. New York: Routledge.

Balibar, E. (1991). Is there a "neo-racism"? In E. Balibar & I. Wallerstein (Eds.), *Race, nation, class: Ambiguous identities* (pp. 17–28). London: Verso.

Balibar, E., & Wallerstein, I. (1991). *Race, nation, class: Ambiguous identities*. London: Verso.

Banton, M. (1988). *Racial theories*. Cambridge: Cambridge University Press.

Behar, R. (1993). *Translated woman*. Boston: Beacon Press.

Behr, M. (1995). *The smell of apples*. London: Abacus.

Beinart, W., & Dubow, S. (1995). *Segregation and apartheid in twentieth-century South Africa*. London and New York: Routledge.

Bennett, D. (1998). Introduction. In D. Bennett (Ed.), *Multicultural states: Rethinking difference and identity* (pp. 1–25). London and New York: Routledge.

Benson, P. (Ed.). (1993). *Anthropology and literature*. Urbana: University of Illinois Press.

Biko, S. (1978). *I write what I like*. San Francisco: Harper & Row. Edited by A. Stubbs.

Bose, M. (1994). *Sporting colours: Sport and politics in South Africa*. Bodmin, Cornwall: Hartnolls.

Bot, M. (1990). *The blackboard debate: Hurdles, options and opportunities in school integration*. Johannesburg: South African Institute of Race Relations.

Bourdieu, P. (1984). *Distinction: A social critique of the judgement of taste* (R. Nice, Trans.) Cambridge: Harvard University Press. (Original work published 1979)

Bourdieu, P. (1990). *The logic of practice* (R. Nice, Trans.) Stanford: Stanford University Press. (Original work published 1980)

Burbules, N. (1997). A grammar of difference: Some ways of rethinking difference and diversity as educational topics. *Australian Educational Researcher* 24(1), 97–116.

Buroway, M. (1981). The capitalist state in South Africa: Marxist and sociological perspectives on race and class. In M. Zeitlin (Ed.), *Political power and social theory: A research annual 2* (pp. 279–335). Greenwich, CT: Jai Press.

Carrim, N. (1992). *Desegregation in coloured and Indian schooling*. Johannesburg: Education Policy Unit, University of the Witwatersrand.

Chalmers, V. (1997). White out: Multicultural performances in a progressive school. In M. Fine, L. Weis, L. Powell, & L. Wong, (Eds.), *Off white: Readings on race, power, and society* (pp. 66–78). New York: Routledge.

Christie, P.(1990). *Open schools: Racially mixed Catholic schools in South Africa, 1976–1986*. Johannesburg: Ravan Press.

Christie, P. (1993). *The future of education in South Africa: School desegregation in the political transition, 1990–93*. Johannesburg: University of the Witwatersrand, unpublished report.

Clifford, J. (1987). Of other peoples: Beyond the salvage paradigm. In H. Foster (Ed.), *Discussions in contemporary culture: Number one* (pp. 121–130). Seattle: Bay Press.

Clifford, J. (1988). *The predicament of culture: Twentieth-century ethnography, literature, and art*. Cambridge: Harvard University Press.

Clifford, J. (1997). Traveling cultures. In J. Clifford, *Routes: Travel and translation in the late twentieth century* (pp. 17–46). Cambridge: Harvard University Press.

Clifford, J., & Marcus, G. (Eds.). (1986). *Writing culture: The poetics and politics of ethnography*. Berkeley: University of California Press.

Cooper, C., Knuckles, F., moby, Owen, F., & Ross, A. (1995). The cult of the DJ: A symposium. *Social Text* 43, 67–88.

Coplan, D. (1985). *In township tonight!* Johannesburg: Ravan Press.

Craik, J. (1994). *The face of fashion: Cultural studies in fashion*. London: Routledge.

Crapanzano, V. (1985). *Waiting: The whites of South Africa*. New York: Random House.

Crime Information Management Centre (1997). The incidence of serious crime during 1996. Detective Service, Head Office, Pretoria, South Africa. Retrieved on January 4, 1998 at http://www.polity.org/za/govdocs/reports/table1gw.html

Cross, M., & Chisholm, L. (1990). The roots of segregated schooling in twentieth-century South Africa. In M. Nkomo (Ed.), *Pedagogy of domination* (pp. 43–74). Trenton, N.J.: Africa World Press.

Dant, T. (1999). *Material culture in the social world: Values, activities, lifestyles*. Buckingham: Open University Press.

David, S. (1996). Social history and cultural paradigms: Modes of thinking identity in South Africa. *Proceedings of the Conference of the Association of University English Teachers of South Africa*, Volume 1, *Southern African Studies*, 22–28.

Davidson, A. (1996). *Making and molding identity in schools.* Albany: State University of New York Press.

Davies, R. (1982). Mining capital, the state and unskilled white workers in South Africa, 1910–13. In M. Murray (Ed.), *South African capitalism and black political opposition* (pp. 173–210). Cambridge, MA: Schenkman Publishing.

Deleuze, G., & Guattari, F. (1987). *A thousand plateaus* (B. Massumi, Trans.). Minneapolis: University of Minnesota Press. (Original work published 1980)

Dent, G. (Ed.). (1992). *Black popular culture.* Seattle: Bay Press.

Denzin, N. (1995). The experiential text and the limits of visual understanding. *Educational Theory* 45(1), 7–18.

Douglas, M., & Isherwood, B. (1979). *The world of goods: Towards an anthropology of consumption.* New York: W.W. Norton.

Dube, E. (1985). The relationship between racism and education in South Africa. *Harvard Educational Review* 55(1), 86–100.

Dubow, S. (1989). *Racial segregation and the origins of apartheid in South Africa, 1919-1936.* London: Macmillan.

Dubow, S. (1994). Ethnic euphemisms and racial echoes. *Journal of Southern African Studies* 20(1), 355–370.

Dubow, S. (1995). *Scientific racism in modern South Africa.* Cambridge: Cambridge University Press.

Dyer, R. *White.* (1997). London and New York: Routledge.

Dyson, A. H.(1997). *Writing superheroes.* New York: Teachers College Press.

Enslin, E.(1994). Beyond writing: Feminist practice and the limitations of ethnography. *Cultural Anthropology* 9(4), 537–568.

Ewen, S. (1988). *All consuming images: The politics of style in contemporary culture.* New York: Basic Books.

Fabian, J. (1990). Presence and representation: The other and anthropological writing. *Critical Inquiry* 16 (Summer 1990), 753–772.

Farred, G. (1992). Unity and difference in black South Africa. *Social Text* 31/32, 217–234.

Farred, G. (1997). The nation in white: Cricket in post-apartheid South Africa. *Social Text* 50 (Spring), 9–32.

Fenster, M. (1991). The problem of taste within the problematic of culture. *Communication Theory* 1(2), 87–105.

Fine, M. (1994). Working the hyphens: Reinventing self and other in qualitative research. In N. Denzin N. & Y. Lincoln (Eds.), *Handbook of qualitative research* (pp. 70–82). Thousand Oaks, CA: Sage.

Fine, M. (1997). Witnessing whiteness. In M. Fine, L. Weis, L. Powell, & L. Wong (Eds.), *Off white: Readings on race, power, and society* (pp. 57–65). New York: Routledge.

Fine, M., Weis, L., & Powell, L. (1997). Communities of difference: A critical look at desegregated spaces created for and by youth. *Harvard Education Review* 67(2), 247–284.

Fine, M., Weis, L., Powell, L., & Wong, L. (Eds.), (1997). *Off white: Readings on race, power, and society.* New York: Routledge.

Fordham, S. (1988). Racelessness as a factor in black students' school success: Pragmatic strategy or pyrrhic victory? *Harvard Educational Review* 59 (1), 54–84.

Fordham, S. (1996). *Blacked out: Dilemmas of race, identity and success at Capital High.* Chicago: University of Chicago Press.

Foucault, M. (1972). *The archaeology of knowledge and the discourse on language* (A. M. Sheridan Smith, Trans.), New York: Pantheon. (Original work published 1969)

Frankenberg, R. (Ed.).(1997). *Displacing whiteness: Essays in social and cultural criticism.* Durham: Duke University Press.

Frederikse, J. (1990). *The unbreakable thread: Non-racialism in South Africa.* Johannesburg: Ravan Press.

Freund, B. (1995). *Insiders and outsiders: The Indian working class of Durban, 1910–1990.* Portsmouth, NH: Heinemann.

Frith, S. (1996). Music and identity. In S. Hall & P. du Gay (Eds.), *Questions of cultural identity* (pp. 108–127). London: Sage.

Geertz, C. (1973). Thick description: toward an interpretive theory of culture. In C. Geertz, *The interpretation of cultures* (pp. 3–30). New York: Basic Books.

Gelder, K., & Thornton, S. (Eds.). (1997). *The subcultures reader.* London and New York: Routledge.

Gilroy, P. (1987). *There ain't no black in the union jack: The cultural politics of race and nation.* Chicago: University of Chicago Press.

Gilroy, P. (1993). *The black Atlantic: Modernity and double consciousness.* London: Verso.

Giroux, H. (1994a). Doing cultural studies: Youth and the challenge of pedagogy. *Harvard Educational Review* 64(3),278–308.

Giroux, H. (1994b). *Disturbing pleasures: Learning popular culture.* New York: Routledge.

Giroux, H., & Simon, R. (1989). Popular culture as a pedagogy of pleasure and meaning. In H. Giroux & R. Simon (Eds.), *Popular culture, schooling, and everyday life* (pp. 1–30). Granby, MA: Bergin & Garvey.

Golan, D. (1994). *Inventing Shaka: Using history in the construction of Zulu nationalism.* Boulder: Lynne Rienner.

Goldberg, D. (1992). The semantics of race. *Ethnic and Racial Studies* 15(4), 543–569.

Goldstein, R. (1983). *The mind-body problem.* New York: Laurel Press.

González, N. (1999). What will we do when culture does not exist anymore? *Anthropology & Education Quarterly* 30(4), 431–435.

Gould, S. (1996). *The mismeasure of man* (Rev. ed.). New York: W.W. Norton.

Grossberg, L. (1989). Pedagogy in the present: Politics, postmodernity, and the popular. In H. Giroux & R. Simon (Eds.), *Popular culture, schooling, and everyday life* (pp. 91–116). Granby, MA: Bergin & Garvey.

Grossberg, L. (1992). *We gotta get out of this place.* New York: Routledge.

Grossberg, L. (1994). Introduction: Bringin' it all back home:Pedagogy and cultural studies. In H. Giroux & P. McLaren (Eds.), *Between borders: Pedagogy and the politics of cultural studies* (pp. 1–25). New York: Routledge.

Grossberg, L. (1996). The space of culture, the power of space. In I. Chambers & L. Curti (Eds.), *The post-colonial question: Common skies, divided horizons* (pp. 169–188). London: Routledge.

Grundlingh, A., Odendaal, A., & Spies, B. (Eds.). (1995). *Beyond the tryline: Rugby and South African society*. Randburg, South Africa: Raven Press.

Gupta, A., & Ferguson, J.(1992). Beyond 'culture': Space, identity, and the politics of difference. *Cultural Anthropology* 7(10), 6–23.

Gupta, A., & Ferguson, J. (Eds.). (1997a). *Culture, power, place: Explorations in critical anthropology*. Durham and London: Duke University Press.

Gupta, A., & Ferguson, J. (1997b). Beyond 'culture': Space, identity, and the politics of difference. In A. Gupta and J. Ferguson (Eds.), *Culture, power, place: Explorations in critical anthropology* (pp. 33–51). Durham and London: Duke University Press.

Gutierrez, K., & McLaren, P. (1995). Pedagogies of dissent and transformation: A dialogue about postmodernity, social context, and the politics of literacy. In B. Kanpol & P. McLaren (Eds.), *Critical multiculturalism: Uncommon voices in a common struggle* (pp. 125–147). Westport, CT: Bergin & Garvey.

Hall, K. (1995). There's a time to act English and a time to act Indian: The politics of identity among British-Sikh teenagers. In S. Stephens (Ed.), *Children and the politics of culture* (pp. 243–264). Princeton: Princeton University Press.

Hall, S. (1981). Notes on deconstructing the popular. In R. Samuel (Ed.), *People's history and socialist theory* (pp. 227–240). London: Routledge & Kegan Paul.

Hall, S. (1986). Gramsci's relevance for the study of race and ethnicity. *Journal of Communication Inquiry* 10 (2), 5–27.

Hall, S. (1991). The local and the global: Globalization and ethnicity. In A. King (Ed.), *Culture, globalization and the world-system: Contemporary conditions for the representation of identity* (pp. 18–39). Binghamton: Department of Art and Art History, State University of New York at Binghamton.

Hall, S. (1992). The question of cultural identity. In S. Hall, D. Held, & T. McGrew (Eds.), *Modernity and its futures* (pp. 273–325). Cambridge, UK: Polity Press.

Hall, S. (1996). When was 'the post-colonial'? Thinking at the limit. In I. Chambers & L. Curti (Eds.), *The post-colonial question: Common skies, divided horizons* (pp. 242–260). London: Routledge.

Hall, S. (1998). Subjects in history: Making diasporic identities. In W. Lubianao (Ed.), *The house that race built* (pp. 289–300). New York: Vintage Books.

Hall, S., & du Gay, P. (Eds.). (1996). *Questions of cultural identity*. London: Sage.

Haney Lopez, I. (1996). *White by law*. New York and London: New York University Press.

Hannerz, U. (1994). Sophiatown: The view from afar. *Journal of Southern African Studies* 20(3), 181–193.

Hebdige, D. (1979) *Subculture: The meaning of style*. London: Routledge.

Hill, M. (Ed.).(1997). *Whiteness: A critical reader*. New York: New York University Press.

Hindson, D., & McCarthy, J. (1994). Defining and gauging the problem. In D. Hindson & J. McCarthy (Eds.), *Here to stay: Informal settlements in KwaZulu-Natal* (pp. 1–28). Durban, South Africa: Indicator Press.

Horrell, M. (1963). *African education: Some origins and developments*. Johannnesburg: Institute of Race Relations.

Howes, D.(Ed.).(1996). *Cross-cultural consumption: Global markets, local realities*. London: Routledge.

Ignatiev, N. (1995). *How the Irish became white*. New York: Routledge.

Issues of rugby and race. (1996, August 24). *The Economist*. Retrieved on December 19, 1996 from World Wide Web: http://sbweb3.med.iacnet.com/infotrac/session/81514/9842560/8?xrn_13.

Jackson, M. (1989). *Paths toward a clearing: Radical empiricism and ethnographic inquiry*. Bloomington: Indiana University Press.

Jackson, P. (1993). Towards a cultural politics of consumption. In J. Bird et al. (Eds.), *Mapping the futures: local cultures, global change* (pp. 207–228). London: Routledge.

Jameson, F., & Miyoshi, M. (Eds.) (1998). *The cultures of globalization*. Durham and London: Duke University Press.

Jeeves, A. (1982). The control of migratory labour on the South African gold mines in the era of Kruger and Milner. In M. Murray (Ed.), *South African capitalism and black political opposition* (pp. 137–172). Cambridge, MA: Schenkman Publishing.

Johnson, A. (1996, August 30–September 6). The crooked cops at the heart of the crime wave. *Mail & Guardian* (South Africa), pp. 4–5.

Johnson, R. W. (1996). Whites in the new South Africa. *Dissent* 43(3), 134–137

Johnstone, F. A. (1976). *Class, race and gold*. London: University Press of America.

Kallaway, P. (Ed.). (1984). *Apartheid and education: The education of black South Africans*. Johannesburg: Ravan Press.

Kallaway, P., Kallway, J., & Sheward, D.(1986). *A bibliography of education for black South Africans*. Cape Town: Education Policy Unit, Department of Education, University of Cape Town.

King, A. (1991). (Ed.) *Culture, globalization and the world-system: Contemporary conditions for the representation of identity*. Binghamton: Department of Art and Art History, State University of New York at Binghamton.

Kirk, P. (1996, August 17). You're offside, Boks! *The Saturday Paper* (Durban, South Africa), p. 1.

Korang, K. (1999). *Locating the west's other in a coeval anthropology: Or, how to read the postcolonial African literary subject/object*. Paper presented at the Unit for Criticism and Interpretive Theory Colloqium Series, University of Illinois at Urbana-Champaign. Urbana, Illinois, September 13.

Kruss, G. (1988). *People's education: An examination of the concept*. Cape Town: University of the Western Cape.

Lather, P. (1991). *Getting smart: Feminist research and pedagogy with/in the postmodern*. New York: Routledge.

Levin, R. (1991). People's education and the struggle for democracy in South Africa. In E. Unterhalter et al. (Eds.), *Apartheid education and popular struggles* (pp. 117–130). Johannesburg: Ravan Press.

Levy, N. (1991). Matching education with employment: Targeting the black labour force. In E. Unterhalter et al. (Eds.), *Apartheid education and popular struggles* (pp. 19–34). Johannesburg: Ravan Press.

Lincoln, Y. & Denzin, N. (1994). The fifth moment. In N. Denzin & Y. Lincoln (Eds.), *Handbook of qualitative research* (pp. 575–586). Thousand Oaks, CA: Sage.

Lipsitz, G. (1994). *Dangerous crossroads: Popular music, postmodernism and the poetics of place*. London: Verso.

Lodge, T. (1984). The parents' school boycott: Eastern Cape and East Rand townships, 1955. In P. Kallway (Ed.), *Apartheid and education: The education of black South Africans* (pp. 265–295). Johannesburg: Ravan Press.

Louw, A., & Sekhonyane, M. (1997). Violence to democracy? KwaZulu Natal's slow road. *Crime and Conflict* 8, 27–33. (South Africa)

Mackay, H. (Ed.). (1997). *Consumption and everyday life*. London: Sage.

Maira, S. (1999). Identity dub: The paradoxes of an Indian American youth subculture. *Cultural Anthropology* 14(1), 29–60.

Mandela, N. (1996, 8 May). Address by President Nelson Mandela to the Constitutional Assembly on the occasion of the adoption of a new constitution. Retrieved on December 18, 1997, from World Wide Web: http://www.polity.org.za/govdocs/speeches/1996/sp0508.html.

Mangan, J. A. (1993). *The imperial curriculum: Racial images and education in the British colonial experience*. London: Routledge.

Manzo, K. (1992a). Global power and South African politics: A Foucauldian analysis. *Alternatives* 17, 23–66.

Manzo, K. (1992b). *Domination, resistance, and social change in South Africa: The local effects of global power*. Westport, CT: Praeger.

Marcus, G., & Fisher, M. (1986). *Anthropology as cultural critique: An experimental moment in the human sciences*. Chicago: University of Chicago Press.

Marks, S., & Trapido, S. (Eds.). (1987). *The politics of race, class and nationalism in twentieth-century South Africa*. New York: Longman.

Marshall, G. (1993). Racial classifications: Popular and scientific. In S. Harding (Ed.), *The racial economy of science* (pp. 116–127). Bloomington: Indiana University Press.

Marx, A. (1998). *Making race and nation: A comparison of South Africa, the United States, and Brazil*. Cambridge and New York: Cambridge University Press.

Mashamba, G. (1990). *A conceptual critique of the people's education discourse*. Johannesburg: University of the Witwatersrand Education Policy Unit.

Massey, D. (1993). Power-geometry and a progressive sense of place. In J. Bird et al (Eds.), *Mapping the futures: Local cultures, global change* (pp. 59–69). London: Routledge.

Massey, D. (1998). The spatial construction of youth cultures. In T. Skelton & G. Valentine (Eds.), *Cool places: Mapping the geographies of youth cultures* (pp. 121–129). New York and London: Routledge.

Matheison, S., & Attwell, D. (1998). Between ethnicity and nationhood: Shaka day and the struggle over Zuluness in post-apartheid South Africa. In D. Bennett (Ed.) *Multicultural states: Rethinking identity and difference* (pp. 111–124). London and New York: Routledge.

Maylam, P. (1985). Aspects of African urbanisation in the Durban area before 1940. In R. Haines & G. Buijs (Eds.), *The struggle for social and economic space in twentieth century South Africa* (pp. 41–62). Durban, South Africa: University of Durban, Westville.

Mazzarella, S. & Pecora, N. O. (1999). *Growing up girls: Popular culture and the construction of identity*. New York: Peter Lang.

McCarthy, C. (1990). *Race and curriculum*. London: Falmer.

McCarthy, C. (1998). *The uses of culture*. New York: Routledge.

McCarthy, C., Hudak, G., Allegretto, S., Mikalucic, S., & Saukko, P. (1999). Introduction—Anxiety and celebration: Popular music and youth identities at the end of the century. In C. McCarthy, G. Hudak, S. Allegretto, S. Miklaucic, & P. Saukko (Eds.), *Sound identities: Popular music and the cultural politics of education* (pp. 1–16). New York: Peter Lang.

McCarthy, C., Rodriguez, A., Buendia, E., Meacham, S., David, S., Godina, H., Supriya, K. E., & Wilson-Brown, C. (1997). Danger in the safety zone: Notes on race, resentment, and the discourse of crime, violence and suburban security. *Cultural Studies* 11 (2), 274–295.

McGurk, N. (1990). *I speak as a white: Education, culture, nation*. Marshalltown, South Africa: Heinemann Southern Africa.

McIntosh, P. (1988). *White privilege and male privilege: A personal account of coming to see correspondences through work in Women's Studies*. Wellesley: Center for Research on Women, Wellesley College.

McLaren, P. (1992). Collisions with otherness: 'Traveling' theory, post-colonial criticism, and the politics of ethnographic practice-the mission of the wounded ethnographer. *Qualitative Studies in Education* 5(1), 77–92.

McRobbie, A.(1994). *Postmodernism and popular culture*. New York: Routledge.

Mercer, K. (1990). Welcome to the jungle: Identity and diversity in postmodern politics. In J. Rutherford (Ed.), *Identity: Community, culture, difference* (pp. 43–71). London: Lawrence & Wishart.

The Mercury (South Africa). (1996, November 26). Less crime over next five years forecast (p.2).

Mncwabe, M. P. (1992). *Separate and equal education: South Africa's education at the crossroads*. Durban, South Africa: Buttersworth.

Mncwabe, M. P. (1993). *Post-apartheid education: Towards non-racial, unitary and democratic socialization in the new South Africa*. Lanham, MD: University Press of America.

Modisane, B. (1965). *Blame me on history*. London: Thames & Hudson.

Molteno, F. (1984). The historical foundations of the schooling of black South Africans. In P. Kallaway (Ed.), *Apartheid and education: The education of black South Africans* (pp.45–107). Johannesburg: Ravan Press.

Morley, D., & Robins, K. (1995). *Spaces of identity: Global media, electronic landscapes and cultural boundaries*. London: Routledge.

Morrell, R. (1996). Forging a ruling race: Rugby and white masculinity in colonial Natal, c. 1870-1910. In J. Nauright & T. J. L. Chandler (Eds.), *Making men: Rugby and masculine identity* (pp. 91–120). London: Frank Cass.

Morrison, T. (1998). Home. In W. Lubiano (Ed.), *The house that race built* (pp. 3–12). New York: Vintage Books.

Nasson, B. (1990). Modernization as legitimation: Education reform and the state in the 1980s. In M. Nkomo (Ed.), *Pedagogy of domination* (pp. 147–178). Trenton, NJ: Africa World Press.

Nixon, R. (1994). *Homelands, Harlem and Hollywood*. New York: Routledge.

Nkomo, M. (Ed.). (1990). *Pedagogy of domination*. Trenton, NJ: Africa World Press.

Ohmae, K. (1995). *The end of the nation state*. New York: The Free Press.

Omi, M., & Winant, H. (1994). *Racial formation in the United States: From the 1960s to the 1990s* (2nd ed.). New York: Routledge.

Owen, K. (1996, December 12). No need for a language laager. *Mail & Guardian* 12(49), 8. (South Africa).

Penny, A., Appel, S., Gultig, J., Harley, K., & Muir, R. (1993). 'Just sort of fumbling in the dark': A case study of the advent of racial integration in South African schools, *Comparative Education Review* 37(4), 412–433.

Perry, P. (forthcoming). *White identities: How white suburban and urban youth make sense of race*. Durham: Duke University Press.

Personal Narratives Group. (Eds.). (1989). *Interpreting women's lives: Feminist theory and personal narratives*. Bloomington: Indiana University Press.

Price, R. (1997). Race and reconciliation in the new South Africa. *Politics & Society* 25 (2), 149–179.

Proweller, A. (1998). *Constructing female identities: Meaning making in an upper middle class youth culture*. Albany: State University of New York Press.

Rabinow, P. (1977). *Reflections on fieldwork in Morocco*. Berkeley: University of California Press.

Rajchman, J. (1995). *The identity in question*. London: Routledge.

Randall, P. (1982). *Little England on the veld: The English private school system in South Africa*. Johannesburg: Ravan Press.

Richards, C. (1999). Live through this: Music, adolescence, and autobiography. In C. McCarthy, G. Hudak, S. Allegretto, P. Saukko, & S. Milaucic (Eds.), *Sound identities: Popular music and the cultural politics of education* (pp. 255–288). New York: Peter Lang.

Richards, J. (1996). *The innocence of roast chicken*. London: Headline Review.

Rizvi, F. (1991). The idea of ethnicity and the politics of multicultural education. In D. Dawkins (Ed.), *Power and politics in education* (pp. 161–195). London: The Falmer Press.

Rizvi, F. (1993). Children and the grammar of popular racism. In C. McCarthy and W. Crichlow (Eds.), *Race, identity, and representation in education* (pp. 126–139). New York: Routledge.

Roman, L. G. (1993). Double exposure: The politics of feminist materialist ethnography. *Educational Theory* 43(3), 279–308.

Rosaldo, R. (1993). *Culture and truth*. Boston: Beacon Press. (Originally published 1989.)

Rutherford, J. (1990). A place called home: Identity and the cultural politics of difference. In J. Rutherford (Ed.), *Identity: Community, culture, difference* (pp. 9–27). London: Lawrence & Wishart.

Sadie, D. (1993). *Model B schools in Johannesburg: The withering of apartheid education or its rebirth?* Unpublished M.Ed. thesis. University of the Witwatersand. Johannesburg, South Africa.

Scott, J. (1995). Multiculturalism and the politics of identity. In J. Rajchman (Ed.), *The identity in question* (pp. 3–12). London: Routledge.

Sisulu, Z. (1986). People's education for people's power. *Transformation* 1, 96–117.

Smith, D. (1998). What is black culture? In W. Lubiano (Ed.), *The house that race built* (pp. 178–194). New York: Vintage Books.

Soudien, C. (1994). Dealing with race: Laying down patterns for multiculturalism in South Africa. *Interchange* 25(3), 281–294.

Soudien, C. (1996). *Apartheid's children: Student narratives of the relationship between experiences in schools and perceptions of racial identity in South Africa*. Unpublished doctoral dissertation. State University of New York at Buffalo.

Soudien, C. (1998). 'We know why we're here': The experience of African children in a "coloured" school in Cape Town, South Africa. *Race, Ethnicity and Education* 1(1), 7–29.

South Africa Institute of Race Relations.(1989). *Race relations survey 1988/89*. Johannesburg: Ravan Press.

South African Institute of Race Relations. (1990). *Race relations survey 1989/90*. Johannesburg: South African Institute of Race Relations.

Stake, R. (1995). *The art of case study research*. Thousand Oaks, CA: Sage.

Steenvald, L. & Sterlitz, L. (1998). The 1995 rugby world cup and the politics of nation-building in South Africa. *Media, Culture & Society* 20, 609–629.

Steinberg, S., & Kincheloe, J. (Eds.).(1997). *Kinderculture: The corporate construction of childhood*. Boulder: Westview Press.

Steyn, M. (1996). *Whiteness just isn't what it used to be: White identity in a changing South Africa*. Unpublished M.A. thesis, Arizona State University.

The third space: Interview with Homi Bhabha (1990). In J. Rutherford (Ed.), *Identity, community, culture, difference* (pp. 207–221). London: Lawrence and Wishart.

Troyna, B., & Hatcher, R. (1992). *Racism in children's lives: A study of mainly-white primary schools*. London: Routledge.

Unterhalter, E. (1991). Changing aspects of reformism in bantu education, 1953–1989. In Unterhalter et al.(Eds.), *Apartheid education and popular struggles* (pp.35–72). Johannesburg: Ravan Press.

Unterhalter, E., Wolpe, H., Botha, T., Badat, S., Dlamini, T., & Khotseng, B. (Eds). (1991). *Apartheid education and popular struggles*. Johannesburg: Ravan Press.

Vally, S., & Dalamba, Y. (1999). *Racism, 'racial integration' and desegregation in South African public secondary schools*. Pretoria, South Africa: South African Human Rights Commission.

Van Rooyen, J. (1994). *Hard right: The new white power in South Africa*. London: I.B. Tauris.

Visweswaran, K. (1994). *Fictions of feminist ethnography*. Minneapolis: University of Minnesota Press.

Walkerdine, V. (1997). *Daddy's girl: Young girls and popular culture*. Cambridge: Harvard University Press.

Williamson, J. (1986). *Consuming passions: The dynamics of popular culture*. London: M. Boyers.

Willis, P. (1990). *Common culture*. Boulder: Westview.

Wilson, R., & Dissanayake, W. (Eds.), (1996). *Global/local: Cultural production and the transnational imaginary*. Durham: Duke University Press.

Wilson-Brown, C. & McCarthy, C. (1995). The organization of affect: Popular music, youth and intellectual and political life. *Discourse* 16(3), 407–422.

Wolpe, H. (1988). *Race, class, and the apartheid state*. Trenton, NJ: Africa World Press.

Wolpe, H. (1991). Some theses on people's education. *Perspectives in Education* 12(2), 77–84.

Wulff, H. (1995). Inter-racial friendship: Consuming youth styles, ethnicity and teenage femininity in South London. In V. Amit-Talai & H. Wulff (Eds.), *Youth cultures: A cross-cultural perspective* (pp. 63–80). London: Routledge.

Yon, D. (2000). *Elusive culture: Schooling, race, and identity in global times*. Albany: State University of New York Press.

INDEX

Achebe, Chinua, *Things Fall Apart*, 53
African National Congress, 12, 23, 26–27, 56
African students: categorization of, 133n.1 (chapter 1), 134n.1 (chapter 4); choosing Fernwood, 43, 106; and class, 37, 86, 89–90; clubs, 58, 68; criticism of African community, 108–109; dancing, 74, 82–83; demographics, Fernwood, 31, 34–35; enforcing taste norms, 81–82; entering Fernwood, 7–8, 17; and fashion, 70–71, 81–82; and globalization, 63; hostility towards, 40, 43; indifference to whites, 105–107; interracial teasing, 86–88; and modernity, 54–55, 63–65; and music, 72–74, 86–87; as Other, 52, 55; planning Deb's ball, 87; and popular culture, 63–65; relationship to South Africa, 12–13, 60; tension with coloureds, 86–89; views on "new South Africa", 55, 57–58, 60, 109; and Zulu identity, 53–55, 63, 72, 86–88. *See also* townships
Afrikaans: in Durban 32; and Soweto uprising, 23
afterparty, 75–76
American popular culture, 2–3, 13, 15, 64–65, 67, 127; in 1950s, 11. *See also* popular culture
Anzaldúa, Gloria, borderlands, 79
Apartheid: and effects, 115–116; and global politics, 10–11; history of,

22–23; resistance to, 23–25, 27; and segregation in schools, 21–23, 29–30, 134n.7; student positions on, 12; weakening of, 23–24
Appadurai, Arjun, 2, 68; scapes, 13–14, 113
Aronowitz, Stanley, 117
Azanian People's Organization, 23

Balibar, Etienne, 10
Bantu Education, 21, 23, 27
Bantu Education Act, 22
bantustans, 21, 24
Bhabha, Homi, third space, 96–97
Black Consciousness Movement, 23
blackness: as a category, 23; containing, 50–51; teachers' construction of, 52–54
border crossing, 17, 96–97, 110, 116; and change, 92–93; coloured students and, 96; and fashion, 17, 102, 105; and music, 17, 85, 99–103, 105; and raves, 91–92; and taste, 17, 92–93, 105–106, 114; teachers' reactions to, 105; and "third space", 96, 97
borderlands, 79, 110
Bourdieu, Pierre, 16, 66–67, 113; critique of, 67; habitus, 16, 18, 66–67, 113–114; habitus, definition, 66; and taste, 2–3, 16–18, 66–67, 113
Burbules, Nicholas, 112, 117–118

case study, 122
Christian National Education, 22–23

Christie, Pam, 26, 28, 30, 134n6
Clase Models, 26
Clase, Piet, 26
class: affinities at Fernwood, 86, 90, 92;
        African students and, 37, 49, 86, 90;
        and the Bantu Education Act, 21; and
        borderlands, 79; and Bourdieu, 66;
        coloured students and, 37–38, 86, 90,
        92; composition, current, 37;
        composition, history, 35; divisions, 90;
        and education, 37; and fashion,
        82–84; and globalization, 13; Indian
        students and, 127, 133n.2 (chapter 2);
        and methodology, 126; race and, 15,
        18, 80; and racial segregation, 21, 80;
        and rugby, 50; and taste, 16–17, 66,
        80, 83–85, 114; white students and,
        35, 37, 48, 80, 84, 127
Clifford, James, 16, 113
clubs, 68–69, 76; African, 68–69, 76;
        and building trust, 125; coloured,
        68, 76, 85, 91–92, 125; and
        connections between students, 85,
        91–92; Indian, 68, 76; violence in,
        58; white, 69, 76
coevalness, 48, 53, 135n.1
coloured students: author's ease with,
        126–127, 130; categorization of, 16,
        133n.1 (chapter 1), 134n.1 (chapter
        4); and class, 37–38, 86, 90, 92; clubs,
        59, 68, 76, 85, 91–92; and
        connections with Africans, 73–74,
        85–90, 92, 98–99; and connections
        with Indians, 38, 86; and connections
        with other students in general, 69, 85;
        and connections with whites, 85,
        89–92; demographics, Fernwood, 8,
        33, 36–37, 106; experience of
        Fernwood, 37–38, 40–41, 86; fashion,
        3, 71–72, 81–82, 97, 101–102, 105;
        gangs, 59; interracial dating, 90, 99,
        105; interracial teasing, 86–87; music,
        72–74, 86, 91, 105; planning Debs'
        ball, 86; on race in South Africa,
        97–99, 101; racism against, 41, 87,
        101, 104, 136n.3; on rainbow nation,
        56; raves, 91–92; relations with

Indians, 38; and segregation/tension
        with Africans, 86–87, 90–92; and
        segregation/tension in general, 69, 80,
        89, 96, 111; and segregation/tension
        with whites, 73–74, 88–89, 98–100;
        speech patterns, 104–105; third
        space, 96–97, 100; and violence,
        58–59
commodities, 65–66, 69–71, 77, 84
"common culture", Paul Willis, 8. See also
        popular culture
Congress of South African Students, 23
Congress of South African Trade Unions,
        25
Craik, Jennifer, 67
cultural studies, 2
culturalism, 10
culture: and apartheid, 75; and
        borderlands, 79; Bourdieu's use of,
        16; commonsense use of, 16; cultural
        essentialism, 1–2, 16, 53–55, 117;
        cultural practices, 16; in cultural
        studies, 2; in educational theory, 1;
        hip-hop, 70, 127; race as, 10, 65, 77,
        105, 113; rave, 71; surf, 71; and taste,
        2; taxi, 135n.4 (chapter 5); Victorian
        understanding of, 20; youth, 63. See
        also popular culture

dating, interracial, 73, 90–91, 105
Davidson, Anne Locke, 110
Debs' Ball, 86–87, 125
desegregation, 7–8, 18; at Fernwood,
        33–36, 55; of schools in South
        Africa, 24–27, 111, 116, 134n.8
downtown. See "town"
Dubow, Saul, 22
Durban: coloureds in, 32; demographics,
        31–32; Indians in, 32; schools in, 7–8,
        17, 34–35, 51, 52; segregation in,
        31–32; "town" 68–69, 71; violence in,
        56–59

educational research: on multiracial
        schooling, 27–29; on race, 112, 116
educational theory, 3–4, 18, 117–118

essentialism: cultural, 3, 16; and difference, 53–55, 117; and identity, 16; and race, 2–4, 16, 117; and taste, 73
Ewen, Stuart, 115

fashion: African students, 69, 70–72, 80, 83; and border crossing, 17, 102, 105; coloured students, 69, 70–72, 97, 101–102, 105; constructing racialized selves, 16–17, 64, 67, 69–70, 72; norms, enforced, 82; South Africa, historically, 11; as a taste category, 67; white students, 71–72, 80, 83; and youth identities, 3
fashion show, 74–76
Fernwood: academic achievement at, 34, 37, 39, 48, 135n.4 (chapter 4); administrative demographics of, 36; administrative uncertainties at, 39–40, 43–45; attraction to black students, 42, 106–107; and class, 35, 37, 39, 49; desegregation of, 8, 33–36, 55; discipline at, 38–40; discourse of standards at, 51–52; discrimination against blacks at, 40–42; history of, 8, 18, 33–36; producing black at, 52–55; producing race at, 18, 47; producing white at, 48–52; racial composition of, 8, 133n.2; recruitment of white students to, 48–49; segregation of students at, 55, 89, 121–122; sports at, 49–51, 106; student demographics of, 36–38; violence at, 58
Fine, Michelle, et al., 116
Frith, Simon, 69

gender: composition of management at Fernwood, 36; methodology and, 126–127, 129–130; and safety, 72; and violence, 58–59
Giddens, Anthony, 2
Gilroy, Paul, 10, 64, 92
Giroux, Henry, 9
globalization: Appadurai on, 2; and class, 13; and culture, 2–3; field of

education on, 2–4; global flows, 13–14, 30; and identity formation, 3–4, 63; and inequality, 13; and South Africa, 3, 10–14, 30. See also popular culture; transnational corporations
Gonzàlez, Norma, 16
Grossberg, Lawrence, 14–16, 115–116
Group Areas Act, 21, 26, 80, 136n.1
Gupta, Akhil and James Ferguson, 112–113
Gutierrez, Kris, and Peter McLaren, 113

Hall, Stuart: defining culture, 1; popular culture as an arena for struggle, 14; racisms, 8, 116; redeploying apartheid, 111–112; shifting discourses of race, 9
Hannerz, Ulf, 11
Hebdige, Dick, 65–66
hybridity, 1, 17, 97–99, 116

identity, 9–15, 114–115; African, 63–65; coloured, 99, 102; and consumption, 135n.2; as essential, 16; global impact on, 10–14; and practice, 15–16; as a process, 16; students actively creating, 15; white, 43, 47–48, 75, 82–85
Indian South Africans: hostile sentiments towards, 38, 83, 98, 126, 136n.3, 136n.4; in Durban, 32
Indian students: and class, 32, 84, 127; and clubs, 68, 76; and dating, 73; Debs' ball, 86; demographics, Fernwood, 7, 36, 38, 90, 136n.6; fashion, 70, 92, 136n.6; fear of violence, 57, 100, 109; and methodology, 126, 134n.1 (chapter 4); music, 72–73, 92–93; racial teasing, 85; relations to coloureds, 38, 91, 96; relation to whites, 91–93; segregation, 123, 97; views on "new South Africa", 57, 61
Inkatha Freedom Party, 56
interracial alliances. See border crossing
interracial dating. See dating, interracial
interracial teasing. See teasing, interracial

Jackson, Michael, 127
job color bars, 20, 133n.1 (chapter 2)

Korang, Kwaku, 135n1
KwaZulu (bantustan), 32
KwaZulu-Natal, 32, 44, 56. See also Natal

Lincoln, Yvonna, and Norman Denzin,
    the fifth moment, 120

Mandela, Nelson, 7, 12–13, 15, 23
Manzo, Kate, 10–11, 22
Massey, Doreen, 13, 63
matric dance, 75–76, 89
McCarthy, Cameron, 18, 117, 133n.2; et
    al., 53, 82
McLaren, Peter, 120
McRobbie, Angela, 14
methodology, 36, 95; and author as
    American, 127–129; and author's
    background, 122; and author's
    preconceived notions of South Africa,
    128; building trust, 124–125; choosing
    Fernwood, 122–123; first impressions
    of Fernwood, 121–122; and method,
    130–131; and methodological frame,
    120–121; and negotiating gender,
    126–127, 129–130; and negotiating
    race, 125–126, 129; questions asked,
    131; and relations with teachers, 123,
    128–130
mission schools, 19–22
modernity: African students and, 54–55,
    63, 65; and race, 17, 63; teachers
    views of, 77
modernization: African students as outside
    of, 54–55; of apartheid, 23–24
Modisane, Blake, 11
Morrison, Toni, 118
music: and African identity, 64–65; and
    border crossings, 17, 85, 99–100, 103;
    conflicts about, 67, 72–76;
    constructing racialized selves, 18, 67,
    74–76, 85–86, 91–92; gangsta rap,
    72, 102–103; rap, 13, 60, 72, 75–76,
    86, 96; raves, 91–93; rhythm and

blues, 72–73, 86–87, 92; and taste,
    67, 72–74, 81, 100–101; techno, 73,
    75–76, 99–100, 102–103; and
    whiteness, 74–76

Natal, 20, 29, 32, 50, 121. See also
    KwaZulu-Natal
nation states 11–12, 48
National Education Crisis Committee, 25
new racism, 10, 22
"new South Africa": black students' views
    on, 60–61; collecting views of, 130;
    criticism of, 99, 101, 109; discourse
    of, 40; optimism, 60–61, 109;
    pessimism, 55–56, 59–60, 102, 109;
    white students' views on, 55, 59–60.
    See also South Africa
Nietzsche, Friedrich, 53
nonracialism, 23, 28

open schools: Catholic 24–25; private, 25,
    134n.6

Pan African Congress, 26
pedagogy, 3–4, 18, 117–118
popular culture, 2, 9, 14–15, 86, 91;
    American, 2–3, 11, 15, 64–65, 67,
    127–128; global, 11, 17, 65, 75, 113;
    scholarship on 14, 133n.5. See also
    American popular culture
Population Registration Act, 21–22. See
    also Race Classification Act
postmodernity: and African students, 63;
    and race, 17, 63, 77
prefects: and methodology, 124; description
    of, 135n.5 (chapter 4)
Private Schools Act, 25

race: after apartheid, 8–9; during apartheid,
    21–24; construction of, 17–18, 80,
    112–118; contradictions of, 114; as
    culture, 10; in educational research,
    2–3, 115–116; essentialized, 2–3,
    9–10, 117; fluidity of, 8–9, 115–118;
    history of term, 10; and identity, 9–10,
    63–65, 76–77, 110, 113–114; and

identity of Fernwood, 47–48, 50–51,
    74–76; and methodology, 125–126;
    and nonracialism, 28; and popular
    culture, 16; production of, black,
    52–55; production of, white, 48–52; as
    a scientific concept, 10, 20; and taste,
    16–17, 63–65, 67, 76–77, 82
Race Classification Act, 21. *See also*
    Population Registration Act
racial categorization: under apartheid,
    133n.1 (chapter 1); in text, 133n.1
    (chapter 1), 134n.1 (chapter 4)
racism, 22, 55–56, 115–116; against
    Africans, 40–41; against coloureds, 41;
    at Fernwood, 40–43, 55–56, 101, 106;
    against Indians, 32, 38, 86, 98, 104,
    136n.3; new, 10, 22; scientific, 22
rainbow nation: author's assumptions
    about, 128; collecting views of, 130;
    discourses of, 23; and Fernwood's
    identity, 48; national appeals to, 55;
    pessimism towards, 55–56; student
    responses to, 55–56. *See also* "new
    South Africa"
Rizvi, Fazal, 117
Rosaldo, Renato, 120
rugby, 40, 49–51, 61, 135n.3 (chapter 4);
    and class, 50; and gender, 52; and
    nation, 50

segregation in schools: before apartheid,
    19–21; collapse of, 24–27; during
    apartheid, 21–23, 29–30, 134n.7;
    students' views of, 40–43, 61
Scott, Joan, 9, 79
Smith, David Lionel, 116
Soudien, Crain, 9, 28–29
South Africa: before apartheid, 10, 17,
    19–21, 92; during apartheid, 7, 11,
    17, 21–24, 27–30, 133n.1 (chapter
    1); in global context, 10–14; as a
    nation state, 12–13. *See also* "new
    South Africa"
South African Democratic Teachers
    Union (SADTU), 43
sports: as identity at Fernwood, 49–51;
    student opinion of, 42

Stake, Robert, instrumental case study,
    122
standards, at Fernwood, 41, 51–52
subcultures, 65–66
"symbolic creativity", Paul Willis, 15,
    65–66

taste: and border crossings, 17–18, 92–93,
    100–102, 106, 114; and Bourdieu,
    15–16, 18, 66–67, 113; and class, 67,
    82–85, 97; codes, enforcement of,
    81–82, 97; codes, resistance to, 81,
    104–105; conflicting uses of, 66–67;
    as distinguished from culture, 3, 16;
    essentialized, 73; fluidity of, 16–17,
    67, 114–115; the force of, 76–77;
    habitus, 16, 18, 66–67; and identity,
    64–65, 135n.3 (chapter 5); and
    interracial alliances, 86–92; and
    popular culture, 17, 64–65, 76–77;
    practices, 16; production of, 115; and
    race, 15–17, 64–65, 67, 77, 113; and
    racialized identities, 72, 82; self-
    expression through, 65–66; and
    separation between races, 77, 92;
    shifting borders of, 67, 92, 110; and
    white resentment, 82–85. *See also*
    fashion; music
taxis, 68, 72, 113, 119, 135n.4 (chapter 5)
teachers: and discipline, 38–39, 43;
    misunderstanding students, 35,
    38–39, 43, 50–51, 53–55; producing
    black, 52–55; producing race, 47;
    producing white, 47; racial
    composition at Fernwood, 36;
    reactions to border crossings, 104; in
    relation to researcher, 123, 128–129;
    responses to desegregation, 43–45,
    112; wanting to leave Fernwood, 44;
    wanting to leave South Africa, 44, 129
teaching race, 117–118
teasing, interracial, 85–88
Things Fall Apart, 53
third space, 96–97
"town", 68–69, 71
townships, 37, 39, 56, 109; excitement in,
    58; representation of, 108; schooling

in, 42; travelling to and from, 37, 39,
   119–120; violence in, 13, 56–58
toyi-toyi, 74, 136n.8
transnational corporations, 12, 77
Tricameral Parliament, 44

uniforms, 37, 51–52, 61, 68
United Democratic Front, 25, 27
United States, students' impressions of,
   59–60, 127–128
Unterhalter, Elaine, 21, 134n.5

violence, 56–59, 103, 109, 115; attributed
   to African men, 57; at Fernwood, 58,
   104; and impact on students' lives,
   56–59; and Inkatha Freedom Party,
   56; in KwaZulu-Natal, 56; statistics
   on, 57; in townships, 13, 56–57

white resentment, 18, 43, 82–85, 103
white students: and African American
   popular culture, 65; and class, 35, 37,
   48, 52, 80, 84, 127; clubs, 69, 76;
   connections with coloured students,
   85, 89–92, 104–105; and dating, 90,
   105; demographics, Fernwood, past, 8,
   31; demographics, Fernwood, present,
35–36, 85; fashion, 71–72, 80, 83; and the
   fashion show, 74–75; fear of African
   violence, 57, 60; friendships with
   blacks, 89; hostility towards African
   students, 42, 74, 82–83, 88; and
   leisure, 68–69; and methodology, 126;
   music, 73, 91–92, 100; and racial teasing, 87–88; and resentment 18, 82,
   84; segregation/tension with
   coloureds, 88–89, 90–92; as valuable
   to Fernwood, 48–49, 52; views on
   "new South Africa", 55, 59–60. *See
   also* segregation in schools; South
   Africa before apartheid
whiteness: and author, 125–126; in Durban,
   31; at Fernwood, 48–52, 61, 112; in
   global context, 48, 75, 125; and music,
   75–76, 101; in South Africa, 134n.2
   (chapter 4)
Williamson, Judith, 66
Willis, Paul, 8, 15; common culture, 15;
   symbolic creativity, 15, 66

youth culture, 65, 67–68

Zulu: as identity, 53–55; stereotypes of,
   29, 53–55, 103, 106